WELLING TO WEMBLEY

A souvenir of Monday, May 25th, 1998 – one more remarkable day in the history of Charlton Athletic

Compiled and written by
ANTHONY FOWLES

with pictures by
STEVE BRIDGE, TONY MITCHELL
and club photographer **TOM MORRIS**

First published in November 1998 by Charlton Athletic Football Company (1984) Limited,
The Valley, Floyd Road, London SE7 8BL. Tel: 0181-333 4000.

Edited, designed and typeset by Rick Everitt.
Production by Corinna Huxley. Additional proofreading by Rachel Kleinman.

Origination by the London Scanning Company Limited,
120 Great Portland Street, London W1N 5PG. Tel: 0171-636 7777.

Printed by Butler and Tanner, The Selwood Printing Works,
Caxton Road, Frome, Somerset BA11 1NF. Tel: 01373 451500.

Charlton Athletic would like to record their thanks to the many supporters who contributed
to this project, regardless of whether their reminiscences or pictures were eventually used.

ISBN 0-9529668-1-6

Dedicated to the Charlton faithful and all football fans who believe the beautiful game is of the people, by the people and for the people.

CONTENTS

Natio
DIV
PLAY-

INTRODUCTION

Charlton's 1997/98 season began in rather less illustrious surroundings than Wembley. It was at Park View Road, on Saturday, July 19th, that goals from Mark Kinsella and Paul Mortimer gave the Addicks a winning start against Welling, if hardly a result to set the pulse racing.

Nine months later, on the morning of May 25th, 1998, that same venue was one of more than a dozen coach departure points for fans travelling to the season's climactic game. Let it stand, in the title of this book, for all the others locally and, as you will read, some rather more exotic locations somewhat further afield.

For keeper Sasa Ilic, Welling to Wembley has a special resonance, since he began his Charlton career in the reserves' 5-2 win over Oxford at Park View Road in late August. And later he played for Welling United in the Conference, before eventually establishing himself as the Addicks' first-choice keeper.

It's no slight on the neighbours, either, to suggest that running out there in the reserves might be considered as low as the season got by some of the other Wembley heroes, too.

It was difficult, in the immediate aftermath of that breathtaking day in May, to quite take in what had happened, never mind revisit it in prose. Yet we were all aware that we had been part of something very special.

When I went to interview him six days before the game, reserve boss Keith Peacock said that if you could choose how to get promoted then the play-offs would always be the preferred option, the "scenic route" as he put it.

You'd naturally aim for the security of finishing in the top two, but if you made it via the play-offs that was better, because then you had the bonus of Wembley. How very right he was.

He also said something else that I later thought astute.

The club had sold 35,000 tickets and there had already been murmurings from those who had been put through the emotional wringer on numerous occasions over the years that their day was somehow being hijacked by the fair-weather brigade.

Keith simply commented that it didn't matter, because people would enjoy the day in direct proportion to what they had put in to the club in the past.

He couldn't for a moment have envisaged, of course, that the game would be so dramatic that even people with no affection for either side would end it in tears.

But if you had enjoyed and endured the ups and downs of the Addicks over three decades or even longer, it was a truly cathartic event. That single afternoon atoned for every humiliation, repaired the damage done by every mistake, down all the years.

It wiped out, at a stroke, the folly of wasting our 1986 return to the top flight after 29 years by being at Selhurst Park.

It guaranteed a massive influx of regular support and restored us, at long, long last, to our historic position of pre-eminence in South East London.

And maybe, if we are honest, it reminded us that football clubs are finally always about their achievements on the field.

The Battle for The Valley was a magnificent enterprise of which we can be rightly proud, but we must not forget that it should never have been necessary in the first place. Similarly, the club has earned and richly deserves its progressive reputation, but that alone was not quite sufficient.

It was perhaps only at Wembley, on May 25th, 1998, that we finally completed our long journey back to credibility and for that we are indebted to manager Alan Curbishley and his heroic players.

If you were like me you got drunk, bought all the newspapers, viewed the video time and again, wallowed in the afterglow. But somehow it wasn't quite enough.

Hence this book.

In the aftermath, some remarkable personal tales came to light, some in The Mercury, others through Charlton Live on Millennium Radio. Many came via the Internet. The germ of an idea planted, I appealed for still more and in they came.

It was my original intention to write them up myself, but a job offer from the football club – which itself was at least in part triggered by the events of May 25th – rendered that impractical.

This turned out to be your good fortune, because former Valley Party candidate Chick Fowles – more recently Garry Nelson's ghost – came sprinting from the subs' bench and far surpassed anything I could have produced.

Inevitably, some offerings have bitten the dust. We have, for example, drawn a discreet veil over the experience of American sports journalist Doug Chapman, who celebrated Sasa's save by bouncing on his waterbed in Somerset, Massachusetts, having shared the agony and ecstasy via Capital Gold on the Internet.

But the reason Charlton is a special club is rooted in the sense of common purpose which unites directors, management, staff, players and fans. That's why our Wembley book is as much about the supporters as what happened on the field. What now unites them all as well is that they never will forget how Charlton brought top-flight football back to The Valley for the first time since 1957.

Rick Everitt

FOREWORD

It was not a classic. When the adrenalin had stopped surging, the blood pounding – if they ever have, if they ever will – calmer judgement had to concede that too many unforced errors, too many downright rickets made the 1998 First Division play-off final less than the ultimate exhibition of footballing finesse.

Less than a classic – and something more as well. Charlton versus Sunderland, Wembley, May 25th, was an absolute belter of a game. An epic. Paradoxically the blemishes – the naff first touch here, the hopelessly underhit pass there, the sleepwalking defence, the misread interception – were major contributors to the game's final heroic scale.

The two hours traffic of open play on the Wembley stage produced several giants and one genius but, all the time, men whose woeful technique had just let them and their teammates down dug deeper to pay back the debt with interest.

There was not one who did not have his moment of rising magnificently to the occasion. Men ran until they could run no more and then, drawing on some reserve tank of the spirit they may not have suspected they possessed, ran and worked still harder.

Skill there was in plenty but, first and last, this was a game about the heart and not the head. About hearts worn with a proud and naked resolution on the sleeve of every player on the field.

It was not, surely, just the final open play score of 4-4 but, as well, this overriding sense of professional passion that shredded the nerves of every spectator present, every viewer and listener; which caused the next day's media to set new benchmarks in superlatives.

"In Charlton's finest hour their manager extracted from them a performance as rich in substance and quality as Wembley can have seen," rhapsodised The Mirror.

And in The Sun, that notorious backer of top dogs and big battalions, John Sadler definitively stated: "Football matches do not come better than this. If there has been one at Wembley these past 30 years, I was not there to see it.

"Even after 78,000 breathless fans had emptied the place last night, I swear the old stadium was still vibrating and echoing from the sights and deafening sound of an epic confrontation."

This book does not seek to recreate the game. Such an attempt would be impossible and is unnecessary. Better than has been granted Blackpool's 4-3 win over nine man Bolton, better than the flickering black-and-white record of England's lonely 1966 World Cup win, the refinements of present-day television – in its visual aspects, anyhow – have left us near perfect blow-by-blow coverage of the play.

Henceforth thousands of lovingly revisited video cassettes will settle bets and sharpen memories made fuzzy by the rosy afterglow: will pull into focus key moments of the live event that were originally blurred by panic, hope and tears.

Rather, this book is intended as a souvenir – a trigger that will call up again the feelings, constantly refresh the emotions, of all the 35,000 fans who made up that great horseshoe of Addick support around one half of Wembley that day of days.

It is the day, in fact, and not the game, which these pages aim to celebrate. The before and after. The inward journey, hoping the best while dreading the worst. The afterwards – the myriad celebrations in despite of total physical and mental wipe-out.

For those whom distance or work or major commitment prevented being bodily at Wembley, this book may go some way towards conveying the welter of emotions experienced first hand.

You were all there in spirit anyway and by an act of easy empathy you – indeed, any football fan – should gain something at least from what follows of the long day's pinballing between the twin towers of triumph and disaster.

Such the intention. And, since it is, this is not a journalist's account but, first and last, a people's history. An Addicks' history. The bulk of what follows is drawn from the letters and first-hand anecdotes of hundreds of Charlton fans.

Inevitably, with so many coming – in every sense – from the same place, many supporters' experiences overlapped.

Hence the account used here from this or that fan must be taken for their own by the dozens of others who took the kind pains to write in with near identical stories.

But equally, plenty of correspondents proved to have "one-off" experiences to relate: not least the significant number who set out for an eventual stroll up Wembley Way from the four corners of the earth.

Come one, come all. Football, God bless it, transcends class, race, wealth, IQ and age. All human life was at Wembley on May 25th, including, as we shall see, those lesser matters of birth and marriage and death.

Perhaps, if we are lucky, what follows will serve not only as a snapshot of a day but of a time in our lives that was suddenly, magically, to relegate the World Cup and the Millennium to the status of perpetual postscripts because, yes, here, now and forever, shared in a common happiness, was and always would be the very time of our life indeed.

BEFORE

GETTING THERE (1): The Locals

Different strokes for different folks. When it comes to getting around we all have our own set ways. Some people are bus people, others train. Some will never surrender the sense of private space and the illusion of being in personal control that a car gives.

Others would much rather ride in a hole in the ground than crawl their way through backed up traffic. A handful think a bike is the only way to fly and, indeed, as we shall come to see, for further flung Addicks boats and planes and Eurostar were essential parts of the getting to Wembley equation. A rickshaw or two may even have been pressed into service.

A huge tranche of supporters, of course, knows that all these forms of transportation are inferior. For people like Neal Target, Jean Tindall, Betty Hutchins, Joyce Moulder, Jean Huelin, the only thinkable way to travel is on the supporters' club coach – thereby to take advantage of the opportunity such a transport of delights allows you for winding yourself deep into the spirit of the game from the moment you climb aboard. A supporters' coach is camaraderie in motion and on May 25th Charlton put no fewer than 114 on the road – all without a hitch.

Since the distant days of the pre-season with its strangely knockabout sense of "promotion or relegation, anything's possible", the team had travelled a tortuous and often torturing path from Welling to Wembley.

Now, give or take a pick-up point, these "club-class" coaches carried some 5,750 Addick supporters far more directly to the same twin-towered destination. With Wendy Perfect immaculate at Mission Control, 79 set out from main branch territory.

Flying the flag

"It was the most we'd ever put on the road," she said. "We did 59 for Old Trafford, but there was never any doubt that record was going to be smashed. What made it really difficult, mind you, was that the 25th was a Bank Holiday, just when the coach companies are at their busiest anyhow. But we're not without clout when it comes to getting their attention."

In fact, Wendy had been given a chance to flex her organising muscles only weeks before when, with a gesture as astute as generous, the Charlton board volunteered to pick up the tab for all the coaches making the run to Port Vale. The offer was snapped up by 2,500 fans who, again over a Bank Holiday, filled a total of 49 vehicles.

Virtue or canniness brought its own reward. By universal consent, relegation-threatened Port Vale were the one side to play the socks off Charlton over the run-in period. But, sustained by the swollen crowd of away supporters, the Addicks somehow clung on.

The Clive Mendonca-converted penalty which settled the game might well have been the product of mass telepathy positively compelling Allen Tankard to trip Danny Mills.

Regarding the Wembley armada, Wendy said: "I can't exaggerate how indebted I am to Dave Evans, Peter Fairclough and Ian Cartwright. They made countless bookings, took the money, made the trips to the bank. Every steward had a parking pass in his or her hand when they boarded their particular vehicle and each one rolled straight on into the coach park with minimum fuss."

Characteristically of the Valley Party club, many of the stewards were simply regulars taking on the good shepherd responsibility on a one-off basis. And doing it well. No one got left behind or lost. The nearest hint of a crisis was averted when Steve Clarke distinguished himself by conjuring up a loo out of nowhere on behalf of one fan with a little – but pressing – local difficulty.

Wagons roll! From a host of rendezvous points with SE postmarks, 79 coaches began a Perfect day at 11.00 hours. But organised by local branches another 35 were already on the road rolling up from Maidstone, East Kent, Sussex and the West Country, with their high-profile allegiance to the Addick cause proclaimed at every window.

No two coaches, naturally, were quite the same. And all were absolutely identical. By right of distance travelled to the pick-up point (more of this anon), let Ian Vagg sum up everyone's experience.

After a champagne breakfast – we thought we would celebrate beforehand, just in case! – eight of us set off for the coach at Abbey Wood.

When we arrived, I and my partner (and no less keen supporter) Deborah Trend were greeted by coach stewards Daphne and Lisa as the "flying the flag for Charlton in Mozambique couple".

Having travelled 6,000 miles, we found this an exceptionally nice welcome. On the way to Wembley we sang and blew up countless red and white balloons.

On arrival at the stadium we lapped up the atmosphere and bantered with the Mackems on the concourse. Then at 13.45 hours we entered the Venue of Legends. Little did we know what was in store.

Neither did anyone else concurrently travelling up for the match in hope, in fear. But not, in the main, in a car.

Given that, whatever the outcome might prove to be, you could pretty confidently predict that the evening would find you drinking yourself either silly in wildest celebration or legless in a vain attempt to drown the deepest sorrow, the prospect of eventually finding yourself at the controls of a vehicle furnished with wheels and requiring steering tended to

Bullish or what?

On me 'ead, son

seem less than alluring.

Nevertheless some strong-minded souls did drive to the game and live to tell the tale from places other than the dock. Debbie Eade and her clan were probably cases in point, typical in all but one respect.

Her breathless account cannot do justice to the magnificent shield-shaped facsimile of a stained glass window (Addick hand brandishing Valiant sword) that her husband had emblazoned, in Boban fashion, on the back of his skull.

Eleven of us (including three generations of Eades) left home at 10am, had a picnic in Wembley car park, took our seats when turnstiles opened to soak up the atmosphere, watched the match (words can't describe), kids gathered autographs after the match, stopped for drinks on the way back and didn't arrive home until 10pm. Brilliant day!

Slam, bam and thank you, ma'am. Route One reporting – and probably about as absolutely average an account as you could come across. But implying one huge point. Once in the stadium, whether they'd come from Darkest Africa or, like the Eades, from Deepest Essex, all fans were equal. The nerve-shattering, nail-biting, larynx-destroying, stomach-churner of an experience that duly unfolded was on totally universal offer.

Most local supporters came by train and tube. Exactly how many we will never know. Steve Rabe's journey must have been utterly typical and can do duty for many other accounts.

I left home at 10am with my brother-in-law and his next-door neighbour, all attired in our Charlton shirts, to catch the train from Bexleyheath. We were hooted at by a number of cars, even a milk

Facing down the enemy

float and one man washing his car wished us good luck. I felt like I was actually one of the players!

The station platform was a mass of red and white and the train was standing room only all the the way to London. We had arranged to meet our friends Vince, Pete and Rick at Charing Cross and, that done, the next port of call was The Griffin where the atmosphere was superb.

Although he was somewhat on loan to the South London contingent, Richard Mehigan's account of his amble Londonwards must also duplicate the experience of thousands.

I'm actually temporarily working (and so living) in Germany at the moment, near a town I confidently expect to return to with Charlton in a year or two, Moenchengladbach.

That's only just inside the Dutch-German border and we actually managed things in quite a civilised fashion that Bank Holiday weekend.

Leaving early for the Channel, Lisa and I were home at my dad's in Bromley by early on the Thursday afternoon.

First order of the day on Monday was depositing the sprog with relatives in Dartford, which is where dad, my brother and I got the train. Catching it made me feel I was really home. It was like putting on an old favourite jacket you'd forgotten you had.

Of course, this particular train wasn't at all a normal one. To all intents and purposes it was a Charlton special. As it came up the line, Albany Park, Sidcup, New Eltham and so on, it got more and more packed, louder and louder, with people of all descriptions, but each wearing Charlton gear.

Consequently, when we arrived at Charing Cross around 10am we found the concourse a sea of red and white. We'd arranged to meet with quite a few further friends coming in on other lines and so, it seemed, had just about every other Charlton supporter in the world.

Pushing for a result

We turned out to be the first of our bunch to arrive and, while I was looking around, I received my first jolt of the day. Those shirts over there were red and white, all right, but with that vertical pattern they really stood out.

Their wearers looked like wasps in a bees' nest and for the first time this morning I was reminded that this was going to be a game of two teams.

One or two hotheads were putting out the word that the police were telling people not to go into Leicester Square as "Sunderland have closed it off". I took this with a very large pinch of salt indeed and, as there was still no sign of our mates, went out across The Strand to the Midland cashpoint.

There was no sign of marauding Mackems trashing the nation's capital but about five of them were queuing in orderly fashion at the above mentioned cashpoint. They looked at me, I looked at them and we all went studiously stonefaced. There was not a suggestion of aggro, but the silence

Early doors

seemed to be going on a bit.

"What time did you leave home then?" I found myself asking the one in front of me.

"Came down yesterday," he replied, in pretty good English. "Stayed with friends. Ought to be a good one this afternoon."

"Too close to call, if we're both honest," I said.

"No way," he said. "If we can hold you with ten, we can beat you with 11."

I shrugged, but afterwards I had the satisfaction of having called it closer than him.

I got my money without being mugged and when I returned to the concourse it was really heaving. It looked like an American election rally. The crowd had got still thicker.

The last of our group finally turned up and we all joined the stream of red and white and green and purple flowing down to the Tube.

Our next immediate pit stop was a pub within striking distance of Finchley Road station where still more friends were due to link up with us.

Refuelling station for another group of Addicks was a flat in the des res enclave of Belsize Park, the home of – shock, horror! – a Norwich fan, Peter Edwards.

Pursuing a career in London (while slowly recuperating from a very rational hatred of Robert Chase) Pete had gravitated to accompanying Addick friends to a number of Charlton games and, on occasion, even been caught red-handed admiring their play.

He had negotiated a deal. In return for a ticket, he would lay on a full monty brunch – egg, bacon, sausage, croissants, orange juice, veggies a speciality – for as many as crossed his threshold.

On the grounds that he was "almost one of us", a group decision was apparently taken that charity should begin at Pete's.

This information comes from Steve Dennard, who duly made his way to the nosh-up from High

Masking their fears

Return trip: two of Charlton's 1947 FA Cup winners, Bill Robinson and Peter Croker, back at the scene of their triumph

Wycombe and discovered that there was a further advantage to the arrangement.

. . . another plus was that the flat was hooked up to cable, so we could watch the pre-match build-up. I'd been pretty peed off by Sky's trailers for the game, which had crudely billed it as a High Noon shoot-out between the two top guns, Kevin Phillips and Clive Mendonca.

I reckoned this was quite an insult to a lot of very talented players on both sides, as well as completely ignoring Super Clive's wonderful ability to lay on chances as often as converting them.

And in a way Sky weren't very consistent. Their trailers promised goals galore, but their studio experts all thought it would be very tight. They agreed that with so much riding on the game all the players would be very uptight and opt to play it safe. They were almost saying it was going to be a dull game.

The betting had finished at Sunderland 8-13 favourites with Charlton at 5-6. Two of the experts, Phil Thompson and Neil Webb, called it that way, predicting a 2-1 win to Sunderland. They seemed to base this on Sunderland being a bigger club, better able to cope with the big occasion.

Garry Nelson, bless his heart, went for Charlton 2-1. But he gave the strong impression that this was his heart overruling his head and he'd come down on the side of the Addicks mainly for old times' sake.

This is well observed. Television soccer gurus are notorious for putting their mouths where the

Shared hopes

production company's money is, but looking at the two 1-1 League draws everyone was saying this had to be another tight one.

Only one person – to leap ahead for a moment – seemed to envisage an alternative scenario.

Interviewed in the bowels of Wembley shortly before the kick-off, somebody called Alan Curbishley pointed out that while everyone was saying "it's going to be an edgy game, a cagey game, if you like", both teams had scored buckets of goals over the season and both liked bombing men forward.

Seven-six on penalties after a 4-4 draw was probably not the precise outcome Curbs had put his mortgage on, but his pre-match reading of the game must have left him more prepared for what was soon to unfold than most.

Of those taking relatively short haul rail journeys to town, one, Tony Warran experienced a moment of history revisited that was definitely not to be sniffed at.

Boarding the train at Hayes station after a morning barbecue at Roger Ford's, we were greeted with this terrible pong like someone had peed in the carriage. Sitting in the corner was Richard Redden.

No, it wasn't that he hadn't been able to contain his excitement. He had a fresh (or not) haddock nailed to a stick which he was waving in front of him. He claimed to be copying the famous Charlton legend.

Not only did he carry this haddock on a stick on the train to Charing Cross, on the tube to Wembley and into the ground, but when I saw him afterwards he was still carrying it. He told me that he was going to preserve it for posterity. Maybe some day it can go into the Charlton trophy cabinet. Or maybe not!

Who more likely than Charlton's dedicated chronicler to remember the old dockers' proverb: "A fish in the hand is worth two in the mush?"

It is a truth universally acknowledged, of course, that, whatever the preferred mode of transport, the journey from the Greater Charlton area to Wembley is one of the most demanding treks known to man. Strict preparation is essential.

Chris Hickey was one of many dedicating his mind to razor-sharp briefing, his body to the most rigorous of work-outs, as the clock ticked remorselessly on.

A perfect 24 hours began in the Royal Oak on the Sunday night when the three Hickey boys joined the assembled listers – The Hong Kong Boys, The Master Brewer, Brian Cassey, Richard Hunt, Jeff Prior, JBR, Mike Stevens, Rick and others whose names I can't remember because I was too drunk.

We were joined by the drummers, the Dundee Boys and, also seeking an orange-free zone, some lads from Holland. The atmosphere was fantastic. It was

Painting the frown red

Matching ideas

like we'd known each other for years. There was so much to talk about; so many stories to tell and listen to. The friendship and camaraderie went far beyond anything else I've known in football.

It's daft but the power of the Internet to create new relationships came alive before our eyes. People who had been names on a screen for the past year were there in living colour.

Being in the Royal Oak with one of the directors, with the listers, the drummers and Rick felt like the most natural thing in the world. But at the same time, it was special. There isn't another club in the country where this could have happened.

I drank the Master Brewer's beer (mighty fine it is too); I finally learned about Yorkeys Knob and about Langwarrin; I heard about the finer points of the Chinese in Hong Kong.

I found out that I had played footie against Richard Hunt in the dim and distant past and that he knows one of my mates well; that Simon Oxley was at school with my brother but neither remembered the other; I found out what Rick does for his day job.

As the song goes: "Oh, what a night!" Fan-bloody-tastic!

My clear and definite prediction was that the game would be dead tight, with neither team giving anything away.

It would be settled by one moment of brilliance or one slip.

It was with sensibilities so keenly honed, judgement so fine-tuned, that many a local Addick took to bed on the eve of the Bank Holiday Monday.

Inflated ideas

GETTING THERE (2): The Exiles

Retirement and the demands of their careers have taken many loyal Charlton fans away from where the mist rolls in from the Thames.

There are supporters now living on the South Coast or in the West Country who remember what the docks were like during the blitz and during their post-World War II heyday. There are 30-somethings now heading up the Blackburn or the Carlisle branch who remember Charlton wallowing around in the Second Division.

All of these wanted to be there on the Whitsun Monday and so many of them were.

Those who didn't hop on their branch's coach made early starts and headed for mainline stations and motorway on-ramps. One with not too far to travel was Gary Crawford.

Being Buckinghamshire-based, I had to travel south on the M1 along with the town of Sunderland.

I had decided to drive to Stanmore and take the Underground to Wembley Park with my son, friend and his son. Stanmore was a sea of red and white stripes and we looked thoroughly conspicuous in our all red shirts.

The Sunderland fans were fantastic. We enjoyed some good friendly banter about the highs and lows of our respective seasons and the prospects for the forthcoming encounter.

On the Tube we got chatting to a Sunderland fan who had flown over from Canada for the game. Before the match we saw pockets of Sunderland and Charlton fans drinking and talking together. What a fantastic atmosphere.

Gary and his party might well have parked next to a soul mate from further north of Watford, Graham Newson.

Driving down from Leeds, the M1 was a daunting sea of Wearside red and white. Stanmore station car park was already full of them by lunchtime and the way up to the stadium was a seething mass of the same.

Inside the mass of Charlton fans was an altogether more comforting sea of red, giving vocally as good as they got. I had speculated in VOTV 76 whether my daughter and I would be back at Wembley for the play-off final after our stadium tour the previous summer and here we were.

Among those coming in by train, third-generation Addick fan Tim Bush may genuinely have the

Full of confidence

Smoke signal

best reason of anyone for remembering the 25th. His letter certainly makes out a case.

I now live in Birmingham – quite a nice place if you can steer clear of St Andrews.

This year Jane and I have been looking forward to our first child whose ETA, despite Jane's ever-escalating expansion, was in mid-June.

As a member I'd secured my Wembley ticket and, other than us losing, nothing could go wrong. Could go wrong . . .

On Sunday, May 24th, Jane started to experience certain pains. She refused to accept my assurances it must be indigestion and off to the hospital we went with me silently praying (a) that this would be a false alarm or (b) our offspring would get his skates on.

The first prayer seemed to be answered. Jane's interior had quietened down and the hospital told us to go home and wait to see how things did or didn't develop. They did. Later on the 24th it was only too clear that there was another customer on the way in through life's turnstile.

Don't quote me, but I have to confess to a measure of divided loyalty. And some apprehension. I didn't get the impression during our second dash to the hospital that Jane was really taking in my instructions to "make it quick".

But she did her best. Our son, as he turned out to be, was born at 2.20 on the morning of May 25th. Although early he was, thank God, in no way premature, but a whopping 8lbs 3oz. I shall always believe he couldn't wait to find out the play-off result.

Around 5.30 I slipped back home for a couple of hours kip and then hurried back to the hospital. Pointing out that she didn't have much on that day, I proceeded to ask Jane's permission to nip off to the game.

Yes, I did ask. One of the reasons I married her is that she's a realist. I'd known all along she'd say Yes. I think.

When, as arranged, I met up with my mates at the designated pub they told me that I was already looking tired and emotional. I replied that I didn't know why because I hadn't had a drink all day but, cheers, a pint or ten of Stella wouldn't go amiss.

As well as Entrances into the Stadium of Life, there are also Exits. The Addick family Watkins, once of Eltham but now living in Canterbury, might dispute with Tim Bush that he holds pole position for remembering Monday, May 25th, 1998.

It could come to a deciding penalty shoot-out, but they have a strong case to argue that their story outdistances anything else experienced by the 78,000 crowd.

As Nicola Watkins, wife to Gary and mother of Jamie and Charlie, sums it up: "It was the worst 24 hours of our lives and the best."

Thirteen year-old Jamie is the family's wordsmith. This is his account.

My mum and dad had taken the Wednesday before Wembley off to drive 75 miles to get our tickets. We were already in a stew because we knew there were

Point of no return

hardly any left. Forty miles up the motorway our car broke down. Now we really started to panic.

The car had to be towed back to Dover, but after loads of phone calls to family and friends in Welling we finally got the tickets sorted and thought we could relax.

On the Sunday night we laid out our Charlton shirts, flags and face-paint and went to bed VERY excited. It was like Christmas Eve – impossible to go to sleep. But I must have.

In the middle of the night, I was woken up by screaming. It was coming from my mum and dad's room. I rushed in and found my brother Charlie had turned blue and stopped breathing. He'd had some kind of fit. We thought he was dying. He's only 11.

My mum was frantic. She called the ambulance. Charlie had swallowed his tongue. I helped my dad release it.

Charlie was still alive. He spent the rest of the night in hospital and had lots of tests and no sleep and we didn't get much either.

We were sure we wouldn't get to Wembley now, but mum said she could look after Charlie so dad and I could go at least. Then Charlie, who seemed back to normal, said he wanted to go and see Charlton too.

The thing was the doctor wasn't going to see him until 10.30. He was on time and by 11 had said Charlie was OK again and could even go to Wembley if he took it easy.

We were all half asleep again, but we all went. When Sasa saved the penalty and the Charlton fans went wild, I cried. But after what we'd all been through the night before, the game didn't seem quite as important as I'd thought it was going to be.

A cynic might say that sending an 11-year old to a play-off final with instructions to take it easy is akin to sending Taricco out at Portman Road with orders to avoid body contact: demanding the impossible. But Charlie suf-

No quarter given

fered no knock-on effects. His mother summed up the all's well that ends well drama with a measure of understatement.

It was certainly a time we will never forget. It cost £1,870 to repair the car and lots more on the day, of course. But it was wonderful that Charlton went up and we're getting season tickets for the Premiership.

Although no further flung than Shirley Park, another dad who, at the end of the day, Brian, owed his by-the-skin-of-his-teeth presence at Charlton's end of the season showdown to his wife's forbearance was Tony Rand.

The beat goes on

A big day was in store for the Rand household. My children had finally got their way and we were set to fly for the first time. With me outvoted on my perennial preference for British resorts, we had opted for a week in Jersey.

I let my wife, Myra, organise things. She had not flown since she was two and was just as excited as the kids.

"All done. We fly out on Sunday," she announced.

"The 24th."

WHOOPS! My face had visibly fallen a mile. A conflict of interest larger than Sasa's thighs now loomed.

"No problem, is there?" my better half responded. "We didn't have anything else planned for that week, did we?"

"Er . . . no, dear."

As the sheer horror of the date clash sank in, my prayers for automatic promotion were delivered with double fervour.

My vocal contribution at matches escalated to unprecedented levels. But as we all know, the incredible string of results wasn't quite enough. It would require the extra games to settle Charlton's destiny.

My 12-year-old son, Matthew, the family's other Addick addict, was equally as aghast at our bad timing. He even expressed the view that defeat by Ipswich would at least mean we wouldn't miss out on seeing Charlton at Wembley.

But we hadn't lost out to Ipswich. Charlton were in the final. And now I was assuring Matthew that he and I would be there too.

"What are you going to do about mum?" was his very fair reply.

"Just leave your mother to me, son," I asserted with a firmness I knew I could never reproduce to her face.

I was seriously concerned. Would this be the one time too many that I had put Charlton first?

Was this the knock-out blow

A big hand for the lads

Hat's final

from which our relationship, first formalised all those years ago when I had dragged her to The Valley to hear our engagement announced over the Tannoy, would never recover?

To Myra's eternal credit my fears were unfounded. She promptly changed our travel plans. She and our 13-year-old daughter Hayley would fly out on the original date, but Matthew and I were rescheduled for Tuesday morning.

Thus somehow I had won the right to get my neck baked over a five-and-a-half-hour stint of queuing for tickets in the Valley sun. When I got home, Hayley sweetly observed that this new red and white look must be part of my Wembley preparations.

Hayley and Myra flew off on the Sunday. For the rest of the day, father and son talked of nothing else but the great day to come.

Little did we know that we would be in the stadium for precisely the same length of time as I had queued for tickets, that we would see 21 goals, that a keeper who had let in ten would cheekily claim to be a hero. And so on . . . and so on.

We had to leave for Gatwick at seven o'clock, but I still made Matthew go out and buy all the papers first.

In Jersey we found that our fame had already spread across the small island. Tour operators, hoteliers and taxi-drivers (one of whom berated me because Sunderland were the poorer by £10 million) were all anxious to sneak a look at the man who had risked breaking up his family to see a football match. Reticence is not necessarily Myra's strongest suit.

No carping, though, could dampen Matthew's or my spirits. It was merely drowned in the jubilant sounds of Charlton's greatest day all still buzzing in our ears.

My thoughts were fixed fast on the Premiership – and, of course, on a wife whose tolerance and understanding, tested way beyond the call of duty, had allowed her husband and son to experience the unbelievable and say: "We were there."

Some you win . . . and some you win again.

GETTING THERE (3): The Expats

Charlton fans are flung further than Edgbaston. There are those in Birmingham, Alabama. Circumstance has scattered dyed-in-the-red-and-white-wool Addicks to the four imaginary corners of the globe.

In May of 1998 not a few of these were intrepidly stiffening their resolve and loosening their bank deposits to set out for the UK and for what their instincts told them would be a "must see" occasion that might never be repeated.

Not just Welling but Wellington to Wembley, as it were.

Let Ian Vagg, last spotted boarding a coach at Abbey Wood with Deborah Trend, speak first for these homing globetrotters.

I had been a regular at The Valley (and Selhurst and Upton Park) for 30 years, but in 1997 I decided to take up the offer of a three-year contract on a customs project in Mozambique.

After I had placed my £5 each-way bet on Charlton for promotion at 40-1 – well, it just had to happen, didn't it? – Deborah and I left England in June.

We planned our first year's three weeks of UK leave to coincide with as many home games as possible and returned in March to see victories over Huddersfield and WBA and the draw against Sunderland. On March 21st we returned to Mozambique.

Our house in the capital Maputo doesn't have the luxury of satellite TV or the Internet, so we are totally dependent on Mercurys, VOTVs, programmes and whatever else is sent out to us by my dad, Henry, and my brother Trevor, both Charlton faithful.

As the season unfolded these mailings carried the ever-clearer message that the dream of a Wembley play-off final was turning into reality. And here were we, having already taken our leave, stranded in South East Africa rather than South East London.

I decided we just had to get back. I can't describe the depth of anxiety that was running through me. All us diehard Addicks have been through our fair share of anxious moments and this was becoming another one for me.

But where there's a will. After much reorganisation, grovelling and favours from colleagues, my release was eventually approved on Tuesday, May 19th. That left four days in which to arrange the flights. Courtesy of South African Airways, we managed to get booked up, the tickets arriving on the morning of the flights.

There are, incidentally, three Sunderland supporters on the project. None of them came home for the match.

At 16.00 hours Maputo time, we left our house for the flight to Heathrow via Johannesburg. At 09.00 hours the next morning we were at mum and dad's in Abbey Wood, safe and sound, though

Departure sign

Predicting a wide-open game

some £1,300 the poorer.

What a risk! Would it all really be worth it? What if we lost? Could we cope? Could we face going back?

All these questions were running through our minds and, of course, we had no idea that the saga had scarcely begun.

Of which more anon.

Around the same time that Ian and Deborah were crossing the equator northwards, Rachel Kleinman was also about 30,000 feet up in the air en route for Addicksville.

Showing a devotion and hardihood that earn her honourable mention here, she had broken into a ten-month sabbatical in Oz by forking out the price of a Chelsea season-ticket on an airfare that would give her a three-week holiday from her vacation with the final as its centre-piece. Rachel is a Pom who whinges with a strict sense of priority, as witness:

I'm so glad to have got back for the game. Australia is wonderful, but can you imagine what it's been like missing the sort of season Charlton have had?

She won't be missing 1998/99.

One thing leading to another, as it does, Rachel found herself being co-opted into doing a little ghosting for The Mercury.

No problem for a former Coopers and Lybrand in-house hack and, indeed, so competent a job did she turn in that she found herself on the receiving end of a decent proposal to join Charlton's Valley staff as the assistant communications manager.

Would she be interested?

Does the Pope dream in Polish?

Rachel, like Ian and Deborah, like Richard Hunt jetting in from Prague ("I've made my life there and I'm happy, but I ache to see Charlton play") had been wrongfooted in respect of Wembley because of the long-term ordering of their lives.

But, as air traffic controllers over the south of England yelled for more benzedrine, there were many more Charlton fans who, lacking faith or the ability to decipher a calendar, came hopping back from short-term holidaying abroad in every possible shade of muck sweat. They had wronged their own feet with bullets entirely of their own despatch.

Unlike Tony Rand, exercising brinkmanship of the most close-cut order, these were the faithful who had not looked before they leapt for vacational therapy. Mark Filer was one who, having painted himself into a millionaire's corner, heroically squirmed his way back out of it.

Pitch invader: Valley announcer Dave Lockwood

About four months ago I was asked by my friend Steve to join him on a Whitsun weekend trip which his company were organising to the Monaco Grand Prix. We'd be coming back on the Tuesday. I accepted like a shot.

It was not until after the Portman Road semi-final leg, when I was saying to Steve what a great result it was as it almost assured us of a trip to Wembley, that he pointed out this would be over the same weekend as the Grand Prix. And, by the way, could I now let him have the money he'd already paid out on my behalf?

The second leg. Charlton 1 Ipswich 0. All right, I can handle success. After a few days of celebrations I booked a one-way flight from Nice (next door to Monaco) to Luton for the morning of May 25th. Nice one. Sorted.

Initial reaction

It wasn't until the conclusion of the 20-hour coach journey out that we were told we would not be staying in Monaco but Marseilles. We would be driven the two-hour journey to the race on Sunday morning.

Not sorted, then. I had a dilemma. I could either travel back to Marseilles after the race and forget the final or I could stay on in Monaco. No contest. While the rest of the group – including the beautiful girl I had met that weekend – rolled off back to the Marseilles hotel, I remained in as close as I have ever got to a state of grace until around ten and then caught a train to Nice Central and a cab to the airport.

I proceeded to spend a very uncomfortable seven hours in the terminal lounge, being woken every hour by the airport police. But my flight left on time and I arrived at Luton at 8am. Now I caught a bus to the train station and a Thameslink train to London Bridge connecting with a mainline service to Charing Cross, where I fetched up at 10 o'clock unfairly looking no different to the hundreds of others who had just come from down the line. I met my brothers and mates and the rest just seems like a dream.

The most memorable thing

Suited to the occasion

about the Monaco end was friend Steve saying. "D'you really think it's worth all the trouble?"

Silly question. Eat your hearts out Steve Martin and John Candy. It was worth every penny spent and every mile travelled to be there on the day when Charlton crossed over the threshold into Premiership football.

Hoping for the best: club secretary Chris Parkes and Addick Steve Sutherland, of the Football League

Universal approbation must also be accorded Dave and Caroline Dowding for, when push came to prioritising shove, doing what a man and a woman's gotta do. They were lying on a beach catching some Portuguese rays, but sad at heart beneath the tan. This holiday was costing them attendance at Wembley.

Even as in silence they separately mourned this malevolent destiny, their waiter, a sadist of pan-European flair, came tripping across the sand chanting "Come on, you Reds!". Something snapped and Dave was on his feet, the scales fallen from his eyes. The waiter's life was spared, but within hours the Dowdings were winging their way back to England and to Wembley.

Mind you, older sweat husbands among the Charlton ranks will wonder how many escudos Dave had to slip the local lad to get a result.

With work commitments running up to August, Russell Taylor was another diehard fecklessly

The shape of things to come: the victorious lads from Bexley-Erith Technical High School for Boys (BETHS), who represented Charlton in a six-a-side warm-up game - the Nationwide Schools Challenge - against counterparts from Sunderland and won 2-1

Coca-Cola
NATIONWIDE SCHOOLS CHALLENGE
CHARLTON ATHLETIC 2
BEXLEY & ERITH TECH HIGH
SUNDERLAND
1
Coca-Cola

Pre-match horse play

pre-positioning himself between a rock and a hard place. But not, as with ever-increasing horror, it was to come to him as the plot sickened, between the Twin Towers on May 25th.

His X-rated experience began, he relates, when his wife Lynn looked up from the holiday brochures to say:

"If you can't make the summer, what about a week in late spring when the kids are on half term?"

"When's that?"

"Whitsun – the week starting May 25th."

"Yeah . . . OK."

Yeah OK is usually my one contribution to these conversations. But this time? As a Charlton supporter your mind doesn't scream out to you: "Hang on, matey, there's football at Wembley in May. You never know what just might happen."

You know what is going to happen. Good start; hang on in the top positions till March; loads of injuries; decline; possibly scrape into the play-offs, but with no real hope. Plus there's my mate Will, a Portsmouth fan, telling me the raison d'etre of both our teams is to finish mid-table in Division One.

I actually believed him. After all, there is a divine right brigade of big-club fans who feel success should be determined by the size of the stadium or the number of trophies you have won in the past. And at the same time there is a body of not small but smaller

Flower power: Les Reed

Here we go, here we go

clubs conditioned to believe that getting good results is just luck. You gear your expectations accordingly. Will's theory was reinforced that week by our 5-2 capitulation at Forest.

Operating in a parallel universe, my mind never put holiday and play-off together until the Boro game in January. The dominance we showed that day against a team we had "no right to beat" now told me there was more than a glimmer of hope.

Or was there? Anyone who was at the Stockport game could not possibly have thought this was Charlton's year. I consoled myself on the way back thinking that I wasn't going to miss out on Wembley, because we weren't going anywhere. The injuries and the decline had started.

The following two-and-a-half months brought the most consistent football I had ever seen from a Charlton side and my career as a soothsayer was over. Instead of seeing us slide down the table, Alan Curbishley ensured that we rose to challenge for automatic promotion.

The play-offs, at the very least, were assured and, given our form, Wembley was more than a dream. It was a distinct hope. When you combine Charlton with hope I get dangerous.

"Ha, ha."

That was Lynn responding to my jokes about flying back from France to see the final. She knows me infinitely better than I know myself and she was looking at me as if to say: "Look, you may genuinely think you're not serious, but I know the seed is there and it's a plant that's going to be deliriously out of control in a few weeks."

Then in March I was made redundant. I got a reasonable package, but you get very frugal when it first happens. Lynn caught the mood.

"You can't really think of flying back from France now."

"No . . . OK."

The issue seemed to have died until I went to the first leg of the semi-finals. The atmosphere among the Charlton fans at Portman Road was the most passionate I had ever experienced and the result was phenomenal. Driving home, I was sure we would win the second leg. I also made the decision there was no way I was going to miss out on Wembley.

Staying in England and joining the holiday on the Tuesday was not an option as I had to drive one of the hire cars. And I'd made another complicating decision. My nephew Ross, already one of the holiday party, must come to Wembley with me. Hmm . . . how best to engineer this little coup?

When I got in after the second leg, Lynn told me that she'd been on the phone to her sister (Ross's Mum) and they had decided that, in view of its importance, it would

Sit down!

be OK for both Ross and me to go to the game. The truth is that Gazza on his way to a kebab stall couldn't have stopped me. But, as it was indeed going to cost us, it was nice to get Lynn's approval of the plan. It was also going to be good to have a travelling companion, because it would be a lonely and depressing journey back if we lost and I really had no idea how it was going to turn out.

For two days I must have won an award for being the Internet's heaviest user as I sorted out the best way to do a South of France-London round trip in a day. I finished up with:

07:30 Toulouse to Heathrow (Air France)

09:30 Arrive Heathrow (maybe kill a few hours with a kip on Ealing Common).

12:30 Make way to Wembley.

20:10 Heathrow to Toulouse.

There was a chance of cutting the return flight a bit fine if there should be extra-time or penalties, but that didn't seem too likely.

The one thing I hadn't really taken on board was the time we would need to get to Toulouse from the house we were renting. It was only after I got there that I realised it would take two-three hours and that this would mean a 4am start for Ross and me.

In fact, the night before, Ross was brimful of excitement at the prospect of an off-the-wall journey and said: "So we make sure we get there, why don't we leave tonight?"

No less brimming with childish excitement myself, I agreed and we left at 1.30 on the Monday morning. The earlier start was inspirational. The journey took us

A wheel pleasure

Anyone know the words to the National Anthem?

nearly four hours. By the time we'd reached Toulouse I was clinging on to more superstitions than when I used to sit on the 53 bus on my way to matches and I had begun to feel that fate was on Charlton's side.

*All went to plan from thenceforward and we got to Ealing about 10am. On the tube we came across a bullsh***ing Sunderland fan giving it: "Just had to buy my boy a watch from Harrods/been looking over properties in Docklands/do you need any World Cup tickets?/staying over for business in the West End."*

I got to wondering whether he was related to Mark Hulyer.

The rest of the day held the same magic for me as for any other Charlton supporter. Somehow it exorcised all the painful memories – in particular the utter lack of ambition at the club in the 70s and early 80s. I raised my arms to Wembley's ageing roof when Ilic saved (well, really it was Gray missing, but who's counting) and I don't think I've ever experienced a similar sense of inner satisfaction as I did at that point.

The timing of the return flight meant we were just able to see Captain Kinsella lift the trophy before we left for Heathrow.

This quick getaway put us among a miserable – no, depressed – crowd of exiting Sunderland fans. One lady saw Ross's CAFC scarf, shook his hand – and promptly burst into tears. To be honest their flat reaction made the victory sweeter. It could have been us.

Many of us have no doubt said to our wives or husbands that this was the SECOND best day of our lives, but do we really mean it? It's not that we love Charlton more than our spouses but that we love them differently and I couldn't say I have ever had the same high as I had on May 25th. Thanks Charlton. We'll remember forever.

So. From near and far, by coach and car, by train and tube and

Bursting to get on with it

Which one's the prince?

plane, by hook or by crook, Charlton got itself to Wembley. Once there it held its breath while singing its heart out and, throughout all the preliminaries – was the result of the schoolboy curtain raiser to prove just a cruel raising of hope on the part of a mocking Fate? Would those naffly suited clones of clowns come up into the stands and start selling double-glazing and insurance? – waited for just one thing. The main event.

Respect! Charlton's Mark Kinsella and Sunderland's Kevin Ball, with referee Eddie Wolstenholme, assistants G Beale and P Norman, plus fourth official Mike Pierce

INTERLUDE

On the eve of Waterloo there was a ball. It was the custom, apparently. On the basis that, come the dawn, you might have your health seriously harmed by cannon ball decapitation, you got a few in. And the rest. On May 25th, Charlton adopted this standard Liege practice.

This time the sound of revelry came not by night, but over lunchtime. While the vast majority of the faithful bobbed down the choppy sea of red and white that Wembley Way had turned into – all the choppier for the disconcerting clash of solids and stripes – the Charlton directors were entertaining friends and saying thank you to scores of support staff in a not-so-little pre-match shindig.

The venue was not the poky bar facilities that are the best to which Wembley can run, but a building scarcely more than a Sasa Ilic punt from the stadium.

Richard Murray has an interest in the Fountain film and television studio facilities just along from the stadium. This would be an excellent place to park and meet and – of course! In a flash of inspiration he realised that on a Bank Holiday the studios would be dark. A big sound stage would make the perfect setting for a glass or three before the game.

It all happened. Within four days Charlton catering manager Dave Archer slammed in the supplies. Guests found the stage replete with a buffet and a bargain basement bar from which the drink flowed like the home win over Middlesbrough.

There may not have been any cameras but there was plenty of action. And, it can now be said, not a little Dutch courage.

Yes, eve of action time. There would be no draw come the afternoon's last kick of the ball. If it were to be Charlton's fate to lose, far better to celebrate what would still have been a splendidly game season, to thank colleagues who had metaphorically run themselves into the ground on the club's behalf, while everyone still had hope in their hearts.

Michael Grade would have felt more at home on the stage than most. The Mercury (well, Peter Cordwell, actually) described him as smiling and trying not to look famous. He was handing out cigars so desiccated as to spark the theory they were his dad's cast-offs.

Steve Dixon – who had done so much classier a job than his Ipswich opposite number in whipping up the semi-final home crowd – was given the PC accolade of smiling "while looking ministerial".

Martin Simons was his usual self – the life and soul of the party. He was doing a great job of masking his anxiety. Knowing he would find the suspense of waiting for the game to start close to unbearable if he were in his seat, he delayed setting off for the stadium until the last moment. And – why not? – after one more pint.

By now the sea of supporters flooding Wembley Way had diminished to a river . . . a trickle. A record gate for any play-off match was already inside the ground. Waiting

DURING

After the rivers and seas of fans kitted out in a fashion to gladden the hearts of Thamesside and Wearside merchandising managers, a river and sea of ink. In an attempt to capture the essence of May 25th, Charlton-Sunderland First Division play-off final on paper, gallons of heliotrope ink have flowed into a sea of purple prose. Or maybe purple haze. The task is impossible. Not even the great Kevin Nolan could hope to do justice to so monumental an occasion.

After two lacklustre cup finals, the game's passion and end-to-end drama – make that melodrama – exploded on to the football following public's consciousness like the ultimate skyrocket. The greatest game seen at Wembley in 30 years, indeed. And why bother to qualify it with that "at Wembley" bit.

Hindsight hardly matters. Those privileged to be there that afternoon know in a way that those absent can never know that being there, living it, suffering it, enduring it, despairing at it, glorying in it, while it was itself a living, breathing, happening NOW event was the most intense minute-by-minute, second-by-second, public experience of their lives. And always to be remembered as being so.

What follows is not offered as a belated effort to replay the game and so, inevitably, muddy those memories. It is, rather, an attempt to set up a few markers that will prompt the reader now to recall, accurately and with renewed freshness, what he or she felt when originally at those heights of ecstasy or depths of despair.

For one that was to end on notes higher than those Maria

Useful experience: Mark Bright (above) and Keith Jones get into the action

Up for it: how the day's unfolding drama looked from the stands

Callas shrilled out when her big toe triggered off the mouse trap, the game started – as hindsight now tells us! – at an already surprisingly elevated level. Both teams immediately vindicated Alan Curbishley's advance reading by setting out to go for it. Play proceeded in a wide and handsome, not necessarily high, way. Yes, the occasion was generating tension, but few of the players seemed that inhibited, when in doubt, about trying something on. Caution, while not exactly thrown to the winds, was not the first item on either side's agenda. What's more, Charlton were getting the better of it.

Probably as many as a third of the Addick "faithful" present were able to tell from direct experience that the game had largely picked up from where the home League game had left off. Though not against a side down to ten men this time, Charlton were coming forward with more edge and looking the livelier. Youds, taking Quinn, and Rufus, looking after Phillips, seemed to have central defensive matters well in hand. It was the Gray-Johnston axis down the left which hinted it might be the sharpest Sunderland threat. But what the hell . . . hadn't the Charlton defence arrived at Wembley with nine straight clean sheets to its collective name? Wasn't Sasa unbeatable?

Maybe not. Dwelling too long over a Youds' back pass, Ilic looked up to discover Phillips all but closing him down. The keeper had no option but to chip with panicked delicacy over the striker's head . . . and almost to the feet of the haring forward Allan Johnston. Ilic hurtled his own bulk outward to block.

He made it, just. And just fairly. The bounce was kind to Charlton and the referee unkind to Phillips when he got lippy over the incident. The Sunderland Echo was later to brand Eddie Wolsthenholme's handling of the game "officious". This is unfair. It is true that he quite speedily flourished three yellow cards, but that seemed to serve his larger purpose. For all that was at stake, there was never the suggestion that a red one might be needed. It was a largely clean game. As the score tends to convince, it flowed. Certainly it never degenerated to the levels of black farce players and spectators suffered in the Portman Road semi-final, where the refereeing was of the quality which brings the game into disrepute.

By midway through the first half, Sunderland were promising to discover a bit of rhythm. The hitherto inconspicuous Phillips was very unlucky to be pulled up by a flag after beating the Charlton offside trap to go clean through. In the 21st minute, Sunderland had a corner on the right and Ball tamely directed a free header he was guilty of not anticipating over the bar. But if Charlton might have been contemplating becoming ragged, a moment of utter quality two minutes later was to reaffirm their sense of superiority.

Aided by Mark Bright's typically astute flick on of Danny Mills' longish throw-in, abetted by Bright's continuing, diversionary run down the inside-right channel, the hitherto inconspicuous

Clive Mendonca had collected the ball with his back to goal, had quarter-hesitated as he quarter-dummied, had turned on a sixpence. The bamboozled Craddock and Williams were reduced to drunken dancing bears clumsily waltzing in each other's arms as, from level with the penalty spot, Mendonca slashed a ball that had never been less than totally under his control past the helpless Perez.

Thirty-five thousand Charlton fans rose as one and a horseshoe half of the Wembley oval was as loud and animated as the other was still and silent. Hugh Murnaghan, an Irish student at Lancaster University and an Addick by long-range osmosis – he had made a first pilgrimage to The Valley just the day before, top man, and been baptised as one of the faithful by the elder brethren of the Royal Oak that very evening – was as joyously lunatic as anyone:

Mendonca scored and everyone went completely berserk. I leapt up and found that my legs appeared to have no strength in them. I had heard of going weak at the knees but had never imagined that I would experience the sensation at a time like this.

We seemed to be cruising as the

One-nil to the Londoners!

Mills and boom

half progressed and it looked that we would manage to put the game beyond opposition who appeared to have left their footballing skills at the Stadium of Light.

But we failed to score the extra goals that would have secured our lead.

Throughout the first half, the singing and chanting from the Charlton end was fantastic, ably marshalled by the superb drummers. I cannot recall having heard the Sunderland fans at all.

For the time in question, at least, this is fair comment. At The Valley for the League game, the Sunderland fans had been the best orchestrated, loudest set of fans of the season. Now, temporarily, their efforts were to be measured on the pipsqueak scale.

To the Londoners 1-0, then, and the assurance bred of those nine clean sheets in a row making the Charlton terraces strangely relaxed. Yes, breaths were taken in sharply when Quinn, who was beginning to find his distant feet, chested the ball down well into the box and it took all of Mark Bowen's experience to get a clean foot in to nick it away.

More panic inhalation was necessary within seconds. From the resulting throw-in, the Sunderland captain fastened on to a loose ball and, as Kevin Nolan described, had "come within a single coat of dubbin on Phillip's right boot of an instant equaliser. The titchy terror popped up at the far post as Kevin Ball's off-target drive skidded past him untouched on its heart-stopping way to safety."

Close encounter: Eddie Youds and Niall Quinn

I'm warning you, the half-time tea here is terrible

Two minutes later, Phillips was crossing from the left. Ilic confounded those questioning his ability on crosses by catching it cleanly, only to have Quinn instantly and only just illegally knock it from his grasp. Should there have been a whistle? The question remains academic, because Eddie Youds – who else? – was long since in calm position on the goalline to tidy up.

Quinn and Phillips again combined to send a square ball across the rampaging forward Lee Clark. The pass came across him in mid-stride. His right-footed snapshot was awkward and, not that much, high.

Finally, in stoppage time being added on to the first half, it was Youds' superb ability to read a game that denied Sunderland an equaliser at the optimum psychological moment. A magnificently timed last-ditch tackle robbed Summerbee as he swept a pass from Clark forward.

The whistle sounded. The Charlton team must have been glad to hear it; Alan Curbishley overjoyed. It is probably fair to say, though, that buoyed up on the knowledge their team had just clocked up 855 minutes of play without conceding a goal, the majority of Charlton supporters enjoyed a half-time in which (false) confidence bordered on complacency. Hugh Murnaghan was inclined to believe the false prophets:

I turned to Talk Radio on my trusty Walkman. The pundits seemed to feel that we had our destiny in our own hands and that Sunderland were there to beat.

Talking to the fellow Addicks around me – people who would have been strangers in any other environment – the feeling was that we would hold on to the lead and even score another goal or two.

When later – much, much later! – the post-match statistics were analysed, they could have been interpreted as justifying this opinion. Sunderland, surprisingly, had enjoyed some 10 per cent more possession of the ball.

Charlton, however, pressing up on Sunderland, had spent some 25 per cent more time in the opposition's defensive third. To make a point through exaggeration, Sunderland were playing with a blunderbuss and Charlton with a rifle. As perhaps, even now, Peter Reid was gently pointing out. It would take only a few more minutes of football to give the relatively laid-back Charlton fans the screaming abdabs.

Niall Quinn's stunning equaliser five minutes into the second half altered the whole psychological balance of the game. It was like a classic left hook suddenly getting a fighter trailing on points back into the reckoning.

When Quinn came arrowing across Youds to bullet the ball down past Kinsella on the near post, it was the Charlton Irishman's sole blemish in an otherwise wonderful exhibition of between the boxes ball-winning, prompting and vision. Now his best defensive effort was no more than a sort of wince.

Quinn shattered that belief which must have been there at the back of the collective Charlton mind: we're impregnable; people don't score against us any more.

On the restart it was the stung

Charlton who swarmed forward to camp for some time around the Sunderland penalty area. Mendonca's bravura holding up of the ball allowed Kinsella to fire in one of his special long-range missiles, but a block sent it for a corner.

When a free kick outside the box allowed him a chance first to feint and then pull a second trigger, a series of ricochets ended only when, from a deflection off Mendonca, Perez had made the nearest thing yet to a genuine save at either end.

The territorial advantage didn't last. Clark was now executing a passable (operative word) imitation of Kinsella and, after the half-time flying saucers, Sunderland were playing, to quote that other Irishman, Mr Murnaghan, "as if Peter Reid had threatened to snog whoever played worst".

Suddenly, from out wide and deep on the left, Clark had pinged a pass in to Niall Quinn, who had pulled off his marker around the corner of the Charlton six-yard box. Quinn chest-trapped and pivoted Mendonca style – and blazed the high bouncing ball over the bar.

Charlton hearts stopped beating and then, resuming, were sorry they had. If their team's attack had come storming back off the ropes, the defence was still rubber-legged.

Keith Jones inevitably lost out in a challenge with Kevin Ball on a 40-60 aerial ball and chance looped it forward to a goal-side Kevin Phillips. Goal-side and onside.

It was Maginot Line time for the latterly impregnable, now sleeping, Charlton defence.

Mark Bowen put up a token arm but, wide out, the excellent view he now enjoyed (or didn't) was not of the linesman's flag rising up but of Phillips enjoying sweet tit-for-tat revenge as he perfectly dinked a shallow lob over the belatedly advancing Ilic.

Two-one to the northerners. Quinn's miss wasn't going to matter. Their single-throated "YESSS!" was the loudest yet and seemed to salute not only the goal, but the fact that the upstarts had been put back down in their place and the natural order of things restored.

It may be South London paranoia but, from this point in the game onwards for quite a long time, this attitude seems to lie not so very latently beneath the surface of the Rob Hawthorne – Alan Brazil commentary.

Despair, not paranoia, was the immediate problem of Charlton fans. Charlie Connelly for one.

I had confidently predicted to anyone who'd listen that there'd be just one goal in it and I felt vindicated when the two other finals that weekend finished 1-0 with the winning goal coming in the first half.

So when we went 2-1 down I was mortified. It was back to the old Charlton, the Charlton who were always caught cold at the start of the second half. We'd blown it, I thought.

I was temporarily seduced by the "Sunderland are a big club and we're not and therefore we've no chance" attitude.

For Ian Vagg, temporarily of Mozambique, the 58th-minute scoreline was even greater cause to slash the wrists.

On the morning I had woken with a premonition. After leading 1-0 at half-time, Charlton would lose 2-1.

Sure enough, having given an accomplished first-half performance the Addicks went in 1-0 up. I really couldn't enjoy the lead. This match meant so much

You what? Sasa Ilic and Niall Quinn exchange pleasantries

Mark Kinsella lets fly

and the premonition was lurking in my mind.

The second half soon brought two Sunderland goals. I was devastated. The premonition was real. I was convinced. It is hard to explain but I reached the point where I was prepared to accept any score so long as it wasn't 1-2. I'm sure if it had stayed that way I was heading for a breakdown.

Past the hour now and Charlton with no option but to chase the game. Apart, though, from Mendonca almost beating the offside trap, the traffic was all one way. The wrong way. It surprised nobody when Curbs now played a familiar card in bringing on Steve Jones. At Wembley, Neil Heaney had played his last game as an Addick.

The departing winger deserves a word. As the temp on the Charlton staff, he inevitably inspired less affection than if he'd been family.

But, brought in by Curbs with what seems like absolutely miraculous foresight on the very eve of Robinson's mid-term injury, Neil Heaney had certainly done a job.

If he'd been virtually missing throughout the action in a couple of games – Port Vale and the away leg at Portman Road – he had turned in useful performances elsewhere.

Generally starting brightly (as in this game: tranquil downstream viewing of the tape shows him getting a surprising amount of change out of Holloway), he went past defenders at times, got over a decent number of good crosses, showed himself surprisingly capable in the air and, when occasion demanded, linked subtly with Mendonca with little one-twos around the edge of the box.

Eddie Youds in commanding form

Suker punch: Mendonca strikes to make it 2-2

That he invariably faded is most probably an interesting insight into the difference between Charlton and Man City fitness/motivation levels.

He faded from the game now to a generous level of appreciative applause, going off to enjoy the rare status of being a player never to lose when wearing a Charlton shirt and, thereby, an imperishable place in the annals of Addick-orientated Trivial Pursuit games.

Two Joneses on for Charlton now and, glory be, as Charlton steadied the ship, combining inside ten minutes of the substitution to vindicate their manager's manoeuvre.

Doubled back into the midfield to scrap in typically dogged fashion, Jones S prised the ball loose and poked it back to Jones K. Dwelling on it minimally, Jonah chipped a longish ball up towards Mendonca. Pythagoras couldn't have come up with a more perfectly calculated arc. Bisecting Super Clive's twin markers exactly, it allowed him to knock the ball sideways into space, accelerate from zero to 60 over two yards maximum and, via a touch on the ball with the sole of his boot that Suker would have given his left foot for, leather it past a no-less-helpless Perez.

From the stands there had seemed an element of hit-and-hope luck about Jonah's chip, but the same tranquil analysis of the tape shows this is to insult the great little man. Four minutes earlier he had delivered as exquisite a ball to his namesake with nearly as joyous a result. He does these things on purpose.

He'd certainly helped Ian Vagg off that hook all of his own pre-

Mark Bowen turns his man

monitory making:

The relief I felt when we equalised could never be equalled, the ecstasy never be surpassed. So I thought. I collapsed on the ground between the seats and lay there trying to compose myself.

With 2-2 showing on the board, the audio balance was now all redialled to the Charlton end. But the big sound engineer in the Sky was once more fingering his knob. Lee Clark had time and space wide on the right this time.

Once again he pinged a cross in to a Niall Quinn peeled away from the nearest marker, Danny Mills. Another and better chest trap, a partial swivel and – bang! – Quinn's favoured left foot had barrelled the ball in at the near post as Ilic arrived too late, Jennings-style, to block the narrow angle. Sunderland back in front. As he adopted the Vagg position, Charlie Connelly was not amused.

When Sunderland immediately went up and scored again, my head dropped so low I ended up looking up the trouser leg of the bloke sitting behind me. Charlton, those bastards, had done it to me again.

They'd built all my hopes up to the point where I'd thought we were finally going to achieve something, only to dash them on the rocks of a leaky defence that had performed so well until today.

Dichio was now on for the shin-splinted Phillips. "Can't be all bad," people said and, by God, it wasn't. Let Kevin Nolan explain.

Hard on the heels of Quinn's brilliant strike followed a point on which this breathtaking game might fairly be said to have turned.

Certainly, if unmarked sub Danny Dichio had met Summerbee's cross from the right with even a modicum of authority, there must have been no way back for Charlton.

Rather than choose to meet a dying cross with a diving header, Dichio chose to hang back and go for a sidefooted volley to a ball that ended being just a shade behind him. The next instant he had scuffed the game's easiest chance into Sasa Ilic's eternally grateful arms.

With more game to chase in much less time, Curbs brought on another attacker for one of that leaky defence. John Robinson on for Danny Mills.

If you still had enough cool left to be analytical, you could actually see an Alan Curbishley team playing, as near as damn it, 4-3-3. Certainly, as Sunderland grew briefly hypnotised by the knowledge that they were holding the lead again, Charlton were pressing. They got a corner. Perez came sailing out to gather safely and blow some wind back into his outfielders' sails.

Within a minute Charlton hearts froze again. From the wing the counter-attacking Quinn found Dichio just two yards out from the Charlton goal and unmarked.

Oh, thank you, God! Thank you, God!

The blessed Mr Wolstenholme had spotted Dichio doing a Van Hooijdonk on Richard Rufus's arm and there was no absolute need to think it was all over just yet.

But there soon would be. Time was running out on Charlton and luck switching sides yet again. In the 84th minute, the mocking goddess poured fresh salt into an old Mark Bright wound.

Another free kick was given just outside the Sunderland penalty area. This time Mark Bowen stood over the ball. As spectators and defenders wondered whether it would be top right or top left Bowen, with intelligent variation, slammed the ball low and hard into the heart of the crowded area.

It was aimed at Bright who diverted it goalwards with a reflex leg-glance. Even more on reflex, Perez used his great upper-body strength and his genius for instant reaction to parry the ball to safety. It was probably all over before he knew it had happened.

Winning a crucial corner: substitute John Robinson

165 games, one goal. But what a moment to score!

It was the one goalkeeping moment in the game matching the high points in the outfield play – and a carbon copy, virtually, of the stunning save Perez had made at The Valley to deny Bright an earlier goal that would have given Charlton two more points and, perhaps, an automatic promotion place. This save could now well have denied them promotion, period.

Sunderland collected themselves for one last series of "no surrender" stands as, the clock now ticking down as at the end of a Sergio Leone Western, Charlton came again.

With just five minutes remaining, Robinson took on Gray in a sprint to the corner flag and won another corner. Charlton's big defenders streamed forward as Johnny-on-the-spot Robbo quickly took the kick high, wide and deep. Perez came sailing out for an encore gather but might as well have been marooned in the north Neasden rush hour, so far short of the ball did he grind to a halt.

14

And from our camera on the other side of the goal . . .

Meanwhile, hanging forever in the air, it seemed, in the ultimate confirmation of the proposition that white men can't jump, Richard Rufus was getting there. His head made unimpeded contact. Taking no more than a couple of gobsmacking centuries, the ball sailed into the unguarded net with the serene majesty of a full moon. With no pretence whatsoever towards serenity, the Charlton end went bananas.

Later Alan Curbishley was to reveal the depths of thought-through planning making the goal inevitable when he explained:

We never expected him to score. We sent him up there to distract them. We hoped someone big would mark him to give the others a chance.

In fact, the plan worked perfectly. As the ball entered the net the entire Sunderland team were seen to be very distracted indeed. Perhaps they were aware that this was the first time that Richard Rufus had scored in 165 first-team appearances and were kicking themselves at not having

Rallying the troops

Performing the hat-trick

nipped round to Ladbrokes before the kick-off.

Rufus's loss of virginity, so to speak, was just one of several landmarks set in the course of the game.

Phillips' 35th strike of the season took the young man, albeit over more games, past Brian Clough's long-standing club record of goals in a season. It had also taken Sunderland's collective total in all matches throughout the season into three figures.

Messrs Connelly and Murnaghan were among the bananas contingent as their respective accounts confirm:

Too drained to go berserk by that point, I had to make do with emitting a strangulated gargle. Then the scoreboard announced that Richard Rufus had scored and I knew I must be hallucinating.

It looked as if we were going to fall at the last hurdle. Then came a corner, Perez was nowhere and suddenly the ball was in the back of the net. I can remember shouting to everyone around me that it was Rufus . . . beautiful bloody Rufus . . . Rufus . . . Rufus . . . Rufus who had scored. The joy was unbelievable and was reinforced when we saw his name up on the Wembley scoreboard.

These two quotes hint at an interesting phenomenon. The endlessly enervating strain of trying to follow the game's myriad pendulum swings even while being hurtled heavenwards and earthwards again on its roller-coaster seems to have blurred many people's ability to see clearly.

Certainly, in the Charlton section furthest from the Royal Box, there were dozens of fans unable to see the newscaster display who were disputing whether it was Rufus or Youds who had nodded the ball home. Well, at first glance the two do sound a lot alike . . .

Sunderland had been within five minutes of the Premiership. The "we had it in our hands but we let it slip" implications of this rippled through their end like the plague.

At the other end, the cocktail of euphoria and sheer surprise had driven the hysteria up to new levels – higher, even, than those reached by Curbishley on his last exuberant sky-rocketing up from the bench.

But to their everlasting credit, the Sunderland players shrugged off the nausea of "so near and yet so far". They went back to the centre and kicked off and the game was still afoot. Euphoria was replaced by fear and trembling and hope and not daring to believe and "how much longer" all the way round Wembley.

By now no watcher could have remained in possession of any impersonal, analytical faculties. Possession belonged to the passions pinballing around the stadium like so many psychic lasers. No one would have been surprised now if the sides had shared six more goals in the last five minutes. But they didn't and the long whistle blast was signalling not another Charlton-Sunderland draw, but the need for extra time.

The management teams came out to rally and regroup. There, bristling with positiveness, was Keith Peacock, the reserves' championship and God knew how many years of commitment to

Running success story

Charlton under his belt.

And there was Les Reed. Lacking his insight into the game's technical and theoretical subtleties, few if any of the watching Charlton fans could accurately say what additional qualities Reed had brought to the training ground over the past three years. All, though, could deliver a final verdict. Whatever the input, it had worked. Pray God it would do so again.

Extra-time began. Within three minutes Charlton hearts beat a little easier; it was easier to catch your breath.

Making another tactical substitution, Curbishley was bringing on English football's best kept secret, Steve Brown, for Bright. A defender for a forward. Bright came off to a standing ovation and, as he would eventually discover, a rave review on the airwaves from Butch Wilkins. To a second crescendo of cheering, Brownie stepped across the touchline. Got problems at the back? Who else you gonna send for?

Ah, the best laid plans of mice and managers . . . Brownie got into the game quickly enough, but instead of impacting on the defence like a jolt of Viagra, his presence preceded by only five or so minutes perhaps its limpest moment.

Gray yet again carried the ball forward into Charlton heartland. His probing diagonal pass forward found Quinn in the centre. One instant touch squared the ball into the inside-left channel and into Summerbee's path.

Summerbee gathered and eluded John Robinson's full-stretch slide tackle from behind in one twisting away move and was through to the edge of the area preparing to pull the trigger.

Finally, after 100 minutes of covering, covering and covering again, Eddie Youds put in a blocking tackle that was half a second too late. Summerbee got his shot off. It sped low and true just inside Ilic's right-hand post – a fine finish to a classically well wrought move.

No! No! No! Whether Charlton fans were now overwrought or underwrought is not worth discussing. For the fourth time they had been dumped on the canvas and, when you've shipped that much punishment, "gutted" is as good a word as any. We've all been there and we all know what it feels like.

Correction. Those who were at Wembley then will know what it felt like this time. They will remember how, shaking their heads clear, they struggled back to their feet to urge their team back into it.

Straws were clutched. It wasn't a Golden Goal situation. There had been yet another kick-off. There were still 20 minutes playing time left. They'd done it twice before. . . The drums began to beat again.

His morning Sky session done and dusted, Garry Nelson had switched from pundit to punter and was just one more face in the crowd. But now he offered up a local opinion.

When Sunderland got their fourth I turned to the people next to me and said that if Reidy's lot allowed themselves to be caught for a third time, they wouldn't deserve to win.

But at the same time, at the back of my mind, something was still saying that Sunderland were so much at sixes and sevens at the back that if Charlton could dig deep enough to come back at them again with purpose and, above all, control, precision, then they weren't out of it yet.

That, as history now records, is exactly what Charlton did. Their midfield seemed to be proclaiming "our turn again, now". Not even the introduction of auld acquaintance Alex Rae – the col-

For the benefit of the bemused

lective shudder that ran through the Charlton horseshoe ("Oh God! Don't let him be the difference!") was almost visible – could prevent them scoring a goal that utterly encapsulated their entire season in miniature.

Gathering the ball on the edge of his own area, Summerbee scampered upfield. He was stopped all but dead in his tracks by the archetypal Steve Brown tackle – crunchingly flat-out, perfectly timed, totally fair, devastating.

The ball spun loose. As typically, Kinsella was first there to pick up the pieces. His fast feet twinkled a diagonal ball into the inside-right channel, perfectly weighted for Steve Jones to run on to it.

Immediately, the covering Gray was on his inside shoulder but, holding him off by sheer strength, Jones steamed straight ahead for the byline. Corner? Goalkick?

Neither. Jones got half a yard's advantage and, as had been his wont all season, crossed a threatening ball hip high towards the Sunderland penalty spot. Mendonca territory! And he was there.

The ball was a little behind him, but killing it all but dead with a backward reaching right foot he left it gently hanging in the air. Then there was nothing gentle going on at all. Another lightning swivel, the right leg recoiling and lashing out full bore and again Perez was helplessly watching the ball scream past his right hand.

Hysteria. Disbelief. Shell-shock. Physical pain. That was just the Charlton section. And, somewhere underneath the monumental collision of emotions, the cool appreciation that, whether their team won or lost, they had been privileged to witness the execution by one of its members of one of the greatest individual performances in soccer history.

Another kick-off. Another whistle. Water bottles being thrown out on to the pitch. Incredibly, still another 15 minutes to play. Oh, please don't let it go to penalties! But please let it be us!

Incredibly, the second period of extra-time was the only phase of the game not to include a goal.

Then here were the men in suits back out on the pitch again, Curbs and Reidy almost more together than opponents for a brief acknowledging moment – here were the subs from the

Coming through: Shaun Newton

Just keep your eyes on the ball

bench, the swapped players back on the pitch, the support staff. Cramped muscles being massaged, some players flopping, others damned if they'd do anything but stay upright. Confusion, milling about. Players of both sides already talking together like old mates, new heroes – and somewhere at the core of it all the question that nobody seemed to have anticipated in full: "Who's up for taking one?"

Martin Simons has a confession to make at this point.

As the Charlton chairman I shouldn't be admitting to this, but when we'd got to the end of extra time, I had a moment of not caring which side won. We'd just come out the other side of an emotional wringer and that wringer had been the most wonderful game of football. Football, pure and simple, was always going to be remembered as the winner at Wembley that day.

I thought I must go and congratulate my opposite number Sunderland chairman Bob Murray before the penalties but, to my regret now, I never got to him.

A bit later, when it came home to me how I would feel reading reports of a match we'd lost next morning in the papers, I realised I'd been a bit overly romantic. I'd have hated it. But there was so much mutual respect in that stadium after two hours play.

Sitting all but opposite Martin Simons was a Charlton fan who was perhaps also experiencing a rather unnatural mind-set. Chick Fowles claims that, briefly, out of all those there, he may have enjoyed a unique status.

As the clock ticked down closer and closer to extra-time, I was living off my nerves as much as anyone. I thought the Sunderland midfield was getting on top near the death and it had to be that if they got a fifth that would be it. With about four minutes to go to the whistle I turned to my son and said: "If it goes to penalties we're going to be all right."

Then the whistle did go and they hadn't scored and, unbelievably, a great sense of tranquility washed over me. All the time they were getting the penalty drill sorted in the middle I was probably the calmest person in the place.

This all stemmed from my being at St Andrews for that very nasty last League match. In the course of it, Sasa made possibly the two best saves I have ever seen in 50 years of watching football. He was absolutely awesome.

Penalties require more than reflex saves and I thought that you had to take Ilic over Perez over a series of five apiece. When Clive wellied the first home I thought: "He's set the hallmark. Just a question of time."

Then it was Sasa's turn. He walked up and tried a pointless bit of gamesmanship at Summerbee's expense, then started all that business of flapping up and down on the line like a vampire seeing the sun coming over the nearest hill.

I thought: "Oh my good Gawd, he's going to blow it. He's the only one who's going to be put off. He won't have any traction for his dives."

Right away I was hot and cold, running sweat all over and as sick at heart, stomach and everywhere else as anybody there.

Ah yes. One little piece of unfinished business remained to be resolved.

THE PENALTIES

The penalty spot on a football pitch is positioned 12 yards forward from the centre of the goalline. The distance between the goal's two uprights is eight yards. They support a crossbar eight feet above the ground.

Stand on that spot – in a local rec, perhaps, or on a school playing field – and the goalmouth looks cavernous. Even with a keeper between the sticks, stuffing the ball away from here has to be a doddle. No probs, mate.

Unless, perchance, you're being asked to do it in front of 78,000 screaming fans and your overriding awareness is that the allocation of an upfront ten million quid or so depends on you hitting the ball home. Wembley is not the local rec.

Alan Curbishley is rumoured to have been miffed that there was no toss to determine which goal should be used for the shoot-out. In jobsworthian mood the authorities had pre-decided on the end closest to the tunnel. In the event of trouble – Wembley is famous for its riots! – the referee would be able to do an easier runner.

This meant Charlton penalty takers must run up to shoot into the teeth of massed Sunderland ill-will. But this might be said to be not necessarily a bad thing and, since Charlton had already emerged victorious in terms of dressing room, first-choice strip and, now, right to lead off the shoot-out, Curbs was arguably asking one favour too many of the Good Fairy.

The stands buzzed. The players and the umpteen support staff to both teams roamed about the centre circle in a kind of focused aimlessness. The two keepers seemed to be avoiding eye contact even as they looked across at each other. Both must have been wished good fortune by a score plus of men who now enjoyed the mixed blessing of not being able to do a single solitary thing about what would soon happen.

Ilic, from a distance, had a distinct look of Peter Shilton about him. For those with memories of one Rome shoot-out, this was less than altogether comforting. Lionel Perez has been brilliantly sketched in Charlie Connelly's pen portrait.

Wasn't Perez a weird shape? All muscles and blond hair, he looked like he'd stepped straight out of one of those computer games where odd-looking characters thrash the hell out of each other in the middle of the street.

It was Perez who was now stepping out to take up his position between the posts. And, as universally expected, Clive Mendonca who was stepping forward from the Charlton cluster.

Truly no problem. Start as you

Don't change your mind! 2-1

mean to go on and... unless... unless. The same thought must have caught in every Addick throat.

Having permitted Super Clive the most sumptuous of hat-tricks, was Fortune now about to say "enough is enough; don't want you too big for your boots" and see that, at the sudden death, he fell flat on his face?

No way. Mendonca's attitude was rock-steady in its lack of self-doubt.

I'd just scored a hat-trick at Wembley. I wasn't going to miss a penalty.

As emphatic as accurate, his strike was an opening declaration of totally confident Charlton purpose. But here came Ilic to face the music. Ignoring the keeper's antics, Nicky Summerbee delivered a strike every bit as compelling. Game on.

Next up for Charlton was Steve Brown – probably (especially with memories of his screamer against Bradford) the "hit man" in the side's roster that most of the faithful would have put their mortgage on.

Brownie points out that he might not have been among their number.

Ten goals went past Sasa . . .

For a start I couldn't be sure whether I'd be on at the end of extra time and I certainly wasn't in any frame that had been worked out beforehand.

Then Les Reed was going around in the centre circle asking who was up for it. When he came to me he had four names on the list. Clive, Jonah, and two of the Marks. The fifth space was still a blank and he was asking me now if I fancied a crack.

I told him "yes", but to bear in mind I'd completely screwed up the last penalty I took, against Wolves. And that was ages ago. And no way did I want to be taking number five, thank you very much, when it would all be coming down to it.

At this point Mark Bowen intervened and said he was quite happy to be the tail-end Charlie and that's what we went with.

Mark might have been vital in tipping the balance at this point. He was going around to everyone saying: "It's ours, I know it. We can do this. We've been on a roll and there's no reason for it to stop now. We won't let it."

He said it in a way that really made you believe it.

All the same, the walk from the centre to the penalty area took me about two hours. All I thought about the whole way was: "Put it to the keeper's right! Don't change your mind! Get it! Put it to the keeper's right! Don't change . . ."

Then I was there and had to do it. I actually preferred shooting in at their end. It helps concentrate your mind. When it's your fans in

Groovy: a fully focused Keith Jones makes it 3-2

front of you, you're so aware of what they're hoping for from you.

But what I think the fans don't realise is the sheer volume of the noise that's coming at you. You literally can't hear the ref blow to signal for you to take the kick. You have to watch him. When his cheeks puff out and then cave in, that's it.

I ran up and hit it and it went nearly where I'd meant it to go. More than good enough. The relief was enormous and I have to confess to a moment of pure selfishness. My instant reaction was: "Got it! Not me! I'm not the one who missed! Some other poor bastard will, but not me!"

It was only when I was on my way back to the middle that it came properly home to me that Charlton were now one ahead again.

But not for long. Allan Johnston. 2-2.

Perez again and . . . Keith Jones. This might have occasioned some moments of disloyal doubting. Addick fans, perhaps without not too much exaggeration, have come to regard the little big man as a thinking man's David Batty.

What the two certainly have in common is a tendency for their goals to seem like exceptions that prove a rule. You don't associate either with pile-drivers from outside the box or lining up behind a dead-ball chance. Perhaps Jonah was a bit lightweight to be going in at number three . . .

Oh, ye of little faith!

As his short steps took him the long way forward, this wasn't Corporal Jones but Denzel Washington's homicidal sidekick "Mouse" in Devil In A Blue Dress. And he wasn't allowing doubt to walk with him.

You can't, of course, replicate the atmosphere, the whole situation of a penalty shoot-out, and in that sense you could say that practice is beside the point. But not entirely.

One day at training, Clive and Mark Kinsella and I got talking and we said: "Look, this could be close. It could well come down to penalties. Maybe we'd better do something about that."

So we stayed out and tried some. What that did for me was let me decide which spot I'd be going for if it did come to a shoot-out. You can't absolutely guarantee you'll be in the groove when it's the real thing, but at least you know what the groove is.

I ended up on the pencilled-in list and since in days of yore I'd taken penalties in anger for Brentford and Southend – no chance at Charlton! – I was happy enough with the idea. My attitude has always been: "If you miss, you miss. But your friends will still be your friends afterwards."

I watched the earlier penalties, but I didn't let them influence me in any way. No monkeying around with bluff and double bluff. The absolute page one of penalty-taking is to decide on that spot and then under no circumstance change your mind. You just keep focusing in on it tighter and tighter.

That's what I was doing as I walked up there and I didn't feel that uptight and the kick went just about exactly as I'd had in mind.

That will do! 4-3

It did indeed. In what was to become a surely unrivalled sequence of spot-kicks – both teams might have been casually compiling a "how to do it" master-class video – Keith Jones's ball to the stanchion on Perez' right was absolutely in the groove. But stress is funny stuff. The fact that this Jonesie didn't panic came, he grins, with a price tag.

Since Wembley I've had about a dozen nightmares. Always the same one. I'm retaking the kick and this time I miss. I always miss. It's really good to wake up then and remember the first one.

Does Kevin Ball have post-penalty nightmares? He shouldn't. Bang! 3-3.

One captain after another. Mark

And suddenly it was over . . .

Kinsella stepped up and, with so distinguished a string of long-range strikes to his credit, seemed almost insulted by this little 12-yarder. To make the whole thing a touch more interesting, he sent Perez the wrong way before curling the ball home.

This was not quite true of Chris Makin, the next man playing catch-up for Sunderland. He went for power and, yes, it worked. But not without a wobble.

The shot was not so very far to the right and not that high. Ilic took off in the right direction and seemed to have chances. He didn't quite get to the right spot at the right time. But, in mid-air, he had picked up the flight of the ball well enough to get his huge left hand, half trailing like a sort of periscope, to the ball. It made a pretty solid contact somewhere around the wrist.

Not quite solid enough. There was enough forward momentum left on the ball for it to squirm away and on into the goal. 4-4.

Mark Bowen next, the volunteer for bringing up the rear and needing now to let his action speak as loud as his words. Which, of course, it did. No messing. With a full bore instep strike he delivered a classic shot to the left top corner and thus obliged Alex Rae not to convert (what a gruesome thought!) but to save the game's first match point.

To his credit – another ten out of ten for courage in the face of the enemy – Rae did exactly that. Ilic had no chance with a fierce shot low to his left. 5-5.

The game was well and truly into sudden death territory now. And the huddles in the centre were hastily forming again to issue new invitations to the dance of sudden death.

John Robinson had been thrown into the maelstrom of the game-chasing second half when less than fully match fit.

Now his tentative, clearly self-conscious approach towards the penalty spot – a walk developing into a twitchy run that then slowed back down to a walk – had all the negative body language you might expect from a player who had positively requested that he not be asked to take a spot kick. Or, at the very least, to be allowed to take one of the first two.

This wasn't wimpishness, he explained, but realism.

Even though I was coming back from a longish break I didn't mind being asked to go from zero to 100 in nothing flat in open play – but a shoot-out penalty was something else. I had taken some in my earlier career – five to be exact. And, no less exactly, I'd converted none. Not the greatest CV in the world.

If you think ahead to the World Cup shoot-outs, you'd have to say that being number six on the list was pretty safe. But the quality of this shoot-out was in a class way above anything managed in France. I think you can say the best we allowed Perez was a quarter chance.

The first ten all went in and I was next up to take one that was pretty much certain to lose it for us if I missed. All right, back to basics. When it went in, the agony before was almost worth the ecstasy.

Niall Quinn was now looking down the match-point barrel. And on a hat-trick of sorts. After his second-half performance, it would have been a very hard-hearted neutral who would have begrudged it to him. Sidefooting rather than smashing it, he put Sunderland level again with what, if everybody watching hadn't known better, might have been

Gray shoots, Sasa saves . . .

thought nonchalance. 6-6.

Is Shaun Newton superstitious? As if he might be, the 13th taker jogged, not walked, to the penalty area. Still wanting to get it over with as speedily as possible, it seemed, he placed the ball on the spot with minimum ado and quick-stepped back no more than three yards. Then fast forward. One, two, thunk! Another side-foot.

Perez guessed and anticipated too well as he dived to his left. The ball had been sent at medium height and speed not that far from where he'd been positioned. Again a trailing arm was extended upwards in the hope of making contact. It didn't miss by much.

But miss it did.

7-6. A scoreline of almost mystic significance to Charlton supporters. But of unbearable tension to Curbishley. As the television cameras recorded for posterity, when the next striker stepped forward, the Charlton boss buried his head in his hands.

An important truth might have been crowding to the front of his mind. Charlton were running out of penalty takers. Rufus, Steve Jones and Youds had all asked not to be put on the spot. Push coming to shove they would have to, but the next man up might be the keeper turned striker . . .

7-6. No doubt there were indeed Addicks who now invoked the ghost of Johnny Summers to hover benignly over Wembley and bless the cause. It would be nice to believe it did. But it is hard to believe that the spirit of anyone once a pro footballer could have wished on Michael Gray what everyone in the country the next morning knew did happen to him.

Gray must have been on every Sunderland supporter's Man of the Match shortlist. And interviewed a couple of months later at cricket's Old Trafford (it made a welcome tea interval change from cataloguing another English collapse) Reid said that he had set his squad to practising penalties and Gray had emerged as the probable top gun.

But this day, the day it mattered, the gun misfired. Somewhere between his approach to the ball and the kick he delivered, there was some split-second drop out, some lesion, between eye and brain, between brain and nerve, between nerve and muscle, between perception and coordination. Who knows what exactly? He did little more than shovel the ball forward. To his credit Sasa Ilic guessed correctly but, that done, half the spectators present could have brought off the save. The strike was that indifferent. To his horror Gray looked up to discover what, a half-second later, everyone else had taken in. He had missed.

And because he had, Michael Gray – no more individually responsible on logical analysis for Sunderland's loss than Quinn (shooting over), Dichio (twice botching great crosses to him close-in), Perez (coming for a corner that Ilic was all but favourite to reach first) – was immediately cast into that outer darkness where dwell all those other spot-kick incompetents and traitors to the cause.

Graziani, Baggio, Baresi, Di Biaggio, Pearce, Waddle, Batty, Ince, Southgate, Aldridge, Cocu, de Boer, and so and so on almost ad finitum. A squad, in short, capable of taking on the world. And one in which Michael Gray would not be a weak link.

Sasa saved.

Gray's eyes shut in that universal instant prayer that he might be allowed to have the moment over again. And for perhaps a third of a second, no one else did any-

As the jubilant keeper races from his line . . .

thing. All around Wembley, two sets of supporters stood wondering whether they should go on believing that they had seen what they thought they might have seen. Then the truth, the awful, the wonderful, the two truths, sunk in.

Around the Sunderland half of the stadium, the sound of an appalled and sickened silence. Across from it – bedlam.

For two and a half hours a cocktail blended of every conceivable emotion – hope and fear and doubt and joy and disbelief and reborn belief and anger and despair and every shade and combination in between – had been ceaselessly, mercilessly shaken.

That single racing heartbeat

They know it's all over

. . . realisation dawns that Charlton are in the Premiership

after Sasa's save, the cork blew from the bottle and relief exploded in a gushing, orgasmic effervescence of undiluted joy. Fathers and sons who might at Christmas exchange a gruff handshake hugged and kissed. Complete strangers hugged and kissed, their respective sexes quite immaterial. Some husbands kissed their wives. Tough, street-wise lads found a shrieking falsetto was all they had left in them. Nearly everyone had tears streaming down their cheeks.

Tears were the one thing the two sets of fans immediately had in common. For the Sunderland fans, the last of the season's wine was flat and sour beyond enduring. Their Charlton counterparts were savouring perhaps the most intoxicatingly champagne moment of their lives. As many have testified.

Brian Duffin: Penalties – watched them all. Couldn't look away. Silent prayers to a God I haven't believed in since I was 15. Ilic has saved! No he hasn't. All five scored for each side. Jeez – I can't bear this!

YEEEEEEESSSSSSSS! Ilic HAS saved! We've won. We're promoted! I can't hear myself think let alone my hoarse voice screaming. The noise, the passion, the sheer bloody relief that it's all over is overwhelming.

Hugh Murnaghan: It's funny how your memory plays tricks on you. From the other end of the ground I remember Sasa diving to his right to save Gray's spot-kick, but watching the highlights later I discovered he'd gone to his left.

A flash of yellow, couldn't see the ball, then suddenly the Charlton bench were hurtling on to the pitch. We'd done it. All the emotions of the day finally caught up with me and I stood on my seat crying like a big girl's blouse. We'd done it! We'd bloody done it!

I'd thought that the ultimate in human pleasure might involve lewd acts with Cindy Crawford. At the end of the game I knew better.

Being The Mail on Sunday's leading sports writer, Patrick Collins (as Chinese whispered to us by his son, Mike) was able to keep a more professional distance on the occasion. Or not.

Although surrounded by Sunderland fans he leapt about five feet in the air. He burst into tears and began hugging me shouting "The Premiership. We're in the bloody Premiership . . . It's the best day ever!"

Objective reportage of the highest order. And a summing-up last thought echoed by many. Perhaps in no more dangerous circumstances than by the very Ian Vagg who, having journeyed with his partner half round the world, now turned to her and declared that this was the best day of his life.

Ross Coomber wrestled with the dilemma facing most grown Addick men with a somewhat greater philosophical rigorousness.

I am 37 (not quite old; not really quite young) and have a son, Jake. His birth was many things but, in all honesty, it is not for me comparable with Monday.

Monday was an event of many emotions taken to their extreme, but if we lost – dare I say it – it was only a football match. If your baby is not healthy it is much more serious and creates a level of concern which, to some extent, blunts the event.

And when the baby is out (if it's your first) you don't really know what to do and start worrying about that. Since this is so, I could "live" the experience of fatherhood with all its ups and downs as fully and completely as possible.

Words cannot describe, though, the intensity of what I was feeling throughout the game and when WE actually won with such courage, strength and resilience – well, I was and still am floating.

It was an event and experience which has rarely been equalled in the sporting (or non-sporting, come to that) world. It was a play-off final, yes, but it became an event and we were there and we won it.

Thus, because it was "only" a football match, I was free to experience it wholesale. And therefore, in a strange way, it was in some senses a bigger experience for me than Jake's birth. It is also a much more interesting video to replay.

On another level I am not sure they can (or should?) be compared. I honestly couldn't be in mind or body any happier than I was the moment we won – but is it comparing like with like?

But why not fuse the two experiences and, defining the one by the other, say that when Ilic saved everything was Jake?

One Eltham couple, meanwhile, combined the communal glee with a purely personal peak. Seizing Charlton's moment, 30-year-old News International computer analyst Ian Amis spontaneously decided to propose to his girlfriend Sarah Downs.

"It was totally unplanned. I didn't even have a ring," he told The Mercury. "It just seemed like the right time."

We might suppose, however cynically, that he knew he was on a winner. At such a moment a girl is hardly likely to respond along the lines of: "My dear Ian, unworthy as I surely am of your fond attention, your declaration does me untold honour. May I express the hope that you cannot be utterly insensible to the sense of gratitude I feel. I am flattered in the extreme.

"There is however a consideration of which you may not be aware that I now feel compelled to draw to your attention. I've currently got this terrific thing going with a gorgeous hunk down the garage so as far as you're concerned it's no way, José, you gotta be joking."

Once Ian had made himself heard and convinced his intended that he was indeed serious, nursery nurse Sarah displayed more sense and sensibility by saying "Yes" and, like the just married Billy Bingham on an earlier Wembley occasion, Ian could be rather more confident than his team that, eventually at least, he would get to score.

While Ian was going down on one knee, others had turned their backs altogether. Incredible or not, this is the manner in which Martin Williamson entered into seventh heaven.

Anyone who thinks the penalties are bad should have tried doing it from underneath the stands!

A group of us, too emotionally drained to stay and watch, congregated by the bar and counted every roar from our end (deafening) and every counter-roar (distant thunder) as the penalties were taken.

At 4-3 there was a massive cheer as it appeared Ilic had saved. This caused us to leap up screaming and shouting. The reality hit almost immediately as the noise quickly subsided.

When Ilic saved from Gray, the sudden roar could be felt as well as heard. We all hugged and sprinted like madmen to join in again.

Didn't they know it was only a game? Mind you, as Members of the Greater Order of Ostriches, they were in good company. Before the eyes of the watching world's cameras, Alan Curbishley had continued to hide his own. Perhaps Shaun Newton's passing flirtation with danger had snapped his last fibre of resolve.

Ironically, it was for the Michael Gray kick that he hid his head in his hands, thus leaving it to tough old rooster Peacock to bellow in his shell-like that Ilic had brought off a save and the Addicks truly, truly, truly were going up.

Ilic's reaction to the save as a save was way over the top, but as a celebration of what it meant for Charlton it was way under. Who was counting when he was

Oi, that's mine!

Prone to celebrate

already being buried under an exultantly headless pyramid of diving teammates and the-all-the way-from-the-bench like greyhounds – “We never doubted!” – management team?

The players were cutting up as daft and soppy as the Addick fans who pushed their bleeding larynxes the extra mile to sustain the incredulous but, yes, we can, we DO believe cheering.

Not a few were later to express their distaste at the thumping in over the sound system of the synthetic victory songs. Here, if ever in time and space, was the moment for the augmented Covered End choir to give “Valley Floyd Road” the ultimate, glorious wellie.

Never mind, there was Mark Kinsella becoming the first Charlton captain to brandish Wembley silverware aloft since Don Welsh in the age of ration books. And here on their half lap of honour was everyone and everybody and all doing silly things. What a lovely bunch of posers!

Only the non-combatants copped out of the en masse Klinsmann impersonations so as not to stain their nice new naff suits. The team saluted the fans and the fans saluted the team and, for a moment, for ever, the bond between them was invisible, the union seamless. Here came Curbs, here was Les. There was no need to go home yet, surely. Why ever go home at all?

All save a handful of totally traumatised Sunderland fans had long since fled the scene. They had begun their thousand mile long journey back from the Stadium of Dark. But let the record show that many had the class to begin with a short detour into the Charlton ranks so as to shake a token hand or two and hope that the last team aboard next season’s Premiership bus didn’t get put off at the next stop.

Similarly, however he might have carried on in the dressing room or in the privacy of his own fly-on-the-wall documentary, Peter Reid was magnificent in public defeat. While he was beyond question both a sadder and a poorer man than when he’d started the day, there seemed no

Moving in for a close-up

Premiership? Straight on

need to cheer him up.

He went straight to Gray to comfort him, was hardly slower in congratulating his opposite number. Not once did he whinge about the play-off system (although surely corners won or a tennis tie-break formula in which there has to be a "guilt-sharing" margin of two would be more just) or sourly remind people that Sunderland had finished two points above Charlton in the League.

Clive Allen had commented on Sky that whichever club lost might find the trauma of "so near and finally nowhere" so demoralising that it would be a spent force in the season to come.

Certainly there are plenty of precedents for such a reaction. Peter Reid, you couldn't help but feel, had made a heroic first attempt to stop any such tendency dead in its tracks.

In a way, wherever fraternising with the enemy took place it was the Mackems who had the easier role. Martin Simons found himself alongside a young Sunderland supporter somewhere in one of Wembley's posh(-ish) backstage parts. His account probably parallels a lot of other people's experience.

She came over and said she felt she must congratulate me – and then she dissolved into floods of tears. I didn't know what to say. Everything that came to mind immediately seemed hypocritical or condescending or gloating. It was if I had intruded on a private grief, was present where news of a bereavement had just been announced. Which in a sense, I suppose, was the case.

Whatever I did say would only make things worse. People in that kind of shock need time in which to start coming to terms with it all. I took my leave as gently as I could and went back to Richard Murray's Fountain Studios. There'd be no Sunderland red there and maybe a Newcastle Brown.

Somebody who is evidently well down the road to stylish recovery is Nic Wiseman. A Sunderland fan, he dwells down among the Southr'on folk and might well have been the first Mackem you clapped eyes on that Monday morning. He put pinky to keyboard on the morrow.

Well, what can I say? What a game! What crap defences the two sides had yesterday. Charlton fans were assuring me prior to the game that they were going to win because their defence was brilliant. Must have been a different one to the lot who showed up at Wembley after half-time.

Sunderland's defence has always been jittery and a one-goal advantage was never going to be enough.

If ever there was a turning point it was when Lionel lunged for a corner ball he had no chance of getting and Richard Rufus (Richard Rufus for Christ's sake – he's never scored before!) headed over him in no man's land. We were only five minutes away!

Then extra-time and penalties. Even then it was hard to separate the two teams. You've got to feel sorry for Mickey Gray. For one of our best players of the season and someone who's Sunderland through and through, that must have been heart-breaking.

The worst thing about all this is that I never wanted this match to happen in the first place. As most people know, I have a great liking for Charlton. I know a load of

Altogether now!

their fans and I even travelled to Wembley with them yesterday.

I've been to The Valley a few times this season, maybe more than a lot of "Charlton fans" who were there yesterday. I want the club to do well. I hope they don't get relegated.

*There's the rub. After Mickey Gray missed that kick I was gutted; really disappointed. But I had nothing to focus my ire on. If it had been any other team, I would be all bloody United/Rovers/City/Wanderers! I hate them. They're full of sh**. I hope they get relegated."*

But I can't do that with Charlton. They are a well-managed club with a great team. It's not fair that I don't even have sour grapes to get me over this disappointment. But get over it I inevitably will.

It's like a bad trip. It's terrible at the time but you know it will go away soon – especially if you get some more of the drug soon. So roll on next season and let's go for the title. And I hope we get to play Charlton in the 1999/2000 Premiership race.

An unsolicited testimonial and nice with it. But local honour demands that we leave the last word in this section to the home team. And the Addicks have had few better spokesmen of late than Garry Nelson. The old lag in him, it seems, gave him a bit more of an overview than most.

I've been asked a couple of times since the game if I feel any disappointment, any bitterness even, at missing out by the odd three years or so on that game at that place.

The honest answer is "No". Partly it's because I'm enjoying what I'm doing now so much. But mainly it's because I was so totally taken up by, so engrossed in, the game itself. What a knee-trembler! It was full of mistakes, but that's one reason it was pure end-to-end excitement.

Of course, the jewel in its crown was Clive Mendonca's hat-trick. If there's ever been a better one, a better technically executed one, it was before my time – which is to say when they still played in elastic-sided boots.

Towards the death the old pro in me didn't want either team to lose and I certainly couldn't bear the thought of anyone missing out with his penalty. The two worst for me to endure were those taken by my old Gatwick Express mates Brownie and Robbo. I had everything crossed when they walked up.

There's another reason why, on a personal level, I was quite relaxed. Common sense tells you that if they'd found a Viagra that works on your knees and by

No doubt now

some miracle I was still on Charlton's books, my chances of getting on would have been slim going on non-existent. Wide left just possibly.

The truth is that the Charlton teams I played in – and some of them were there or thereabouts for a play-off place – weren't in the same class as this one. Same league, I'll have to say now.

I do think we were part of the whole process whereby Charlton pulled itself up and away from oblivion. The squad was better when I left than when I arrived and I think we established a series of camps on the side of the mountain that was climbed today.

The only negative thought I had today relates to me reaching a play-off final with Brighton and not then getting the nod even for the bench. I've got over that now but seeing them in the background today I couldn't but feel sorry for Sweaty Balmer and Chappie and, in a different way, Mike Salmon.

Every Charlton supporter knows that they all put it in for the club time after time – often when, unlike today, there wasn't a trace of glamour or glory in the air. Whether it's at The Valley or not, they are all worthy of and capable of good futures in the game.

The team today – the team that evolved over the last quarter of the season – has a sharper cutting edge than the ones I was involved in. It's technically better – more craft and skill. It's faster at the back. Above all, it's acquired the priceless quality of resilience. It's got steel running through it now. It's a team that believes in itself. And that's why I think they're in with a better than even shout of keeping their feet away from the Premiership trap door next spring.

Don't ever tell Curbs I said so, but he's bought well these past months and today is a day he can say it all came together.

Hey, Curbs . . !

And now for those of you who may have come in late, here's Richie with a summary of the day's play. Sorry, in place of Richie Benaud, here's Charlton director Bob Whitehand.

Just back from Portugal. What a week! Left for Portugal Sunday; dropped the family off on holiday – then up at 4.45am to drive to Faro and catch 07.00 flight.

Just made connection thanks to wonderful Portuguese British Air

Unlucky Phil Chapple enjoys the moment

lady checking me in at gate. Arrived Heathrow 11.00; met rest of family; off to Wemberlee. Several things stick in my mind.

1. Unbelievable atmosphere pre-match at Richard Murray's studios.

2. Walking up Wembley Way with my 74-year-old mum reminiscing about my dad; how much he would have loved it.

3. Standing on the balcony with a huge lump in my throat as I watched a sea of Charlton supporters coming up Wembley Way.

4. Fireworks as the teams came out. Lump in the throat again.

5. Clive's fantastic first goal. Kissing my father-in-law.

6. Half-time. Will it be ten clean sheets in a row? Large drink.

*7. Niall Quinn's first goal. Oh sh**!*

*8. Phillips scoring. Oh sh** again.*

9. Clive equalising. Kissed my father-in-law again and two other directors, I think.

10. Quinn scores again. Cannot repeat language I used in Charlton-sanctioned publication. Prayed to God and my dad for second equaliser.

11. Prayers answered. Rufus scores. I couldn't believe it. He doesn't even score in training. Father-in-law is kissing me, though, so it must be true. Proceed to kiss everyone who wants a kiss.

12. Extra-time. Summerbee! Where did he come from? Damn! We're down again. Lots of praying and talking to my dad One last push, guys.

13. Clive again! It's his hat-trick! Lips now chapped from kissing everyone in my vicinity.

14. End of extra-time. Penalties! Loo a necessity. On way back bump into Jane Murray. Two large vodkas later we have calmed ourselves (ha!) ready for the shout-out.

15. Don't miss, Robbo. Leg stands up to pressure as does his heart. Gray hits it low. Sasa down and saving it. All is a blur of hugs, kisses, handshakes, crying. We are UP!

I congratulated all my fellow directors in the box, all the coaching staff, playing staff, backroom staff (especially Peter Varney), partied all night with them and flew back to Portugal next morning on the 8am flight.

The only people I didn't get to thank were our fantastic supporters – what a noise, what a support! You were a vital part in a fabulous jigsaw that all came together and lifted us to the Premiership. Now we need to stay there and show London that there's a force to be reckoned with south of the Thames.

It's true, you see. Money isn't everything.

Mention of Peter Varney affords us, courtesy of Brian Cole, the perfect instance of realpolitik with which to leave Wembley and begin coming – after many delays and digressions – literally back down to earth.

Peter relates: Sasa had just saved the Gray penalty and we were in the first moments of joy when I felt a tap on my shoulder. It was Colin Powell. "Peter," he said. "Does this mean I can have a new mower?"

Steve Jones tells it like it was

Mike Salmon congratulates Danny Mills and Sasa Ilic

MESH

AFTERWARDS

When you were a kid you used to go out to play and every evening go through a whole mish-mash of childish and not so childish emotions.

Then suddenly it was time to go home. Your mum would be calling or the shadows would be longer than you could remember seeing before. Or between two steps you felt played out and knew that you'd had enough. You came in from the rec, the park, the street next to yours, the bomb site. Until the next time, the endless game was over.

So it was for the Charlton fans at Wembley. The players had done their last silly, celebratory things; the overkill sound system had long since stopped its audio gate-crashing; and for the first time in hours you were clocking how you yourself felt. Tired.

And the rest. It was time to follow the long since departed Sunderland supporters back into the wide, wide world.

Its tidal flow reversed, the former rapid, buoyant flood towards Wembley was now an almost currentless backwater. The mounted police had used their horses to construct a series of locks so that, containing the thousands upon thousands of spectators between each pair of gates, they could drip-feed the crowd into Wembley Park station in Tube-size chunks.

The conditions were perfect for a swing bowler – hot, overcast, humid. It was the sort of weather in which you get hot under the collar. But, all passion nearly spent, this crowd was patience personified. They had just received a gift that they would treasure for ever and they were still full of gratitude, still trying to take in the wonder of it. The sense of occasion was enormous. It was like a long time ago when you still believed that kings and queens were special and you waited uncomplainingly for hours to catch a glimpse of one complacent wave.

Voices were low, sporadic. It was easy to pick up fragments of conversation from a fair distance away. Somebody said that Sutton and Mendonca should spearhead England's World Cup campaign. It was possibly fatigue but nobody gave him an argument.

Mendonca was the one word to recur and recur. Comparisons were beginning to be made and the two benchmarks he was regularly being bracketed with were Romario and Muller. Everybody knew that with his close control capable of wrongfooting tight, Continental-style defenders, Mendonca should be in Hoddle's World Cup squad.

Dream on. Everybody knew he wouldn't be. If the play-off final

Memories are made of this

YES!

NO!

had been a month earlier. . . The crowd shuffled forward another 50 yards and something became crystal clear. People had begun the amiable debate which will last for as long as there are two Charlton supporters left on the face of the earth. Which of Mendonca's goals was the best?

Another shuffle forward. One older man was suddenly half fainting, but the inevitable doctor present, Bill Almond (down from Chorley as the beneficiary of his son-in-law's reverse nepotism and don't you ask him who his first team is), shepherded him through the immediately parting crowd and, where there was a hint of fresher air, got his instant patient sorted.

Another shuffle. Another wait. Few people had either energy or appetite to buy from the still open junk-food stalls. At last!

You were stepping out, through the tunnel, up the ramp and into the station. The train was in before you could say John Robinson – and then it really hit you. The slump into near stupor was universal.

Coming down slowly

The ride to Baker Street was bad. The renewed queuing through the tortuous out-the-station, back-in-the-station route the uniforms had devised ("it's for your own safety, sir") was enervatingly worse.

Worst were the long waits, the stop-go slogs down the line in the trains leaving – finally! – Charing

Robbo cup

Cross. The oven-like carriages were as packed as in the morning. But whereas then they had been vibrant with great expectation, bubbling with chat, now they were as much a study in still life as a doctor's waiting room. People sprawled like so many fish cast up on a beach by a great wave.

It was the same on the coaches. There was scarcely a hint of "kiss me quick" charabanc high jinks on the drag back to South London and Kent. Ray – surname withheld to protect the thick-witted! – was yet another victim of booking a family holiday over the Bank Holiday weekend.

After a longish day in the New Forest boondocks, he was driving his family back to their Gillingham home, desperately fiddling to tune his car's dodgy radio to a wavelength that would give him the result.

Suddenly, before he had managed to cut through the static, there coming towards him was a convoy of East Kent branch supporters' coaches. Ray needed only one glance at the lifeless faces of the passengers, as ashen and tight-lipped as Ron Knee ever achieved, to deduce the worst.

"Oh, God. We've lost," he announced.

And for many, having lost was almost what it truly felt like. Celebration should have been the order of the day and, yes, the homing instinct was drawing the majority of Addicks back to their local patch for the drink-up to end all drink-ups.

But after that afternoon of non-stop action, a balancing reaction was taking its toll. There were many who, the video once running, never rose from their besotted, hypnotised slumpdown on the living-room couch. As for living it up, tomorrow was another day.

Partial party-poopers were the men most entitled to be so, the players. To say thank you, win or

My turn to hold it

Strike force

lose, for a monumental year, the club had arranged a formal reception out at Heathrow's Excelsior hotel for the squad and key officers.

Around 200 attended and all the makings for a night of whoop-dee-do seemed to be in place. But as Mark Bright was to try to get across to Radio Four's predictably obtuse sports correspondent next morning, as far as the players were concerned, the well had finally run dry.

The two hours of flat-out contesting everything, the brain-pulverising suspense of the penalty contest, the surge into new stratospheres of jubilation, had finally drained the last drop of adrenalin out of the day's heroes. Their get up and go all gone, they now politely got up and went.

Look what we've got!

You couldn't say they hadn't earned their shut-eye. And for their part, they knew that what they had won together and now bound them together in an exclusive brotherhood could henceforth be celebrated at any time – just whenever they chose to revisit it in memory.

But – "get a grip!" – as the evening went through the gears into the dark, there were many who, gaining their second wind, knew that the day having been Charlton's, the night was still Young's. Or Bod's, or Beck's, or whatever they hadn't run out of yet.

At Blackheath, the Princess of Wales might also have set a capacity crowd record. Once you'd finally got in at the bar, the trick was to buy at least three rounds. The overspill on to the heath outside was prodigious and the stimulus provoking countless drivers to give an "I'm with you" hoot.

Car horns sounded throughout the outer SE postal districts this evening – and across quite a few DA ones, too – but the fortissimo epicentre had to be here.

It was cabaret time, too, for anyone who cared to watch. Spreading away from the Princess as far as the eye could make out through the darkness were umpteen small-sided pick-up football games with red shirts doing their damndest against red shirts.

The able-bodied, still partially sober, Charlton faithful had been inspired to pay their heroes the most direct of tributes. On every hand, imitation was showing itself the highest form of flattery – and the mere faintest of resemblances.

Getting in some training for a Tuesday lunchtime session in the Royal Oak, Phil Burch, over especially from Boston, Mass, was one of the multitude outside the Princess.

So, too, eventually, was a dweller even further afield, Brian

Crowning glory

Chain . . .

Cassey, earlier one of Martin Simon's guests at the pre-match party in Richard Murray's studios.

Made the present of an air ticket all the way from Australia by his wondrously sympathetic partner, Brian had bludged a match ticket out of Martin over the Oz to Pomland phone and duly seen history being made first-hand. Then, as he relates, he found himself recipient of a bonus.

One of the highlights for me was at Charing Cross on the way home. On seeing my Charlton shirt, two gentlemen, one an Arsenal supporter, the other Brighton, insisted they buy me a pint to celebrate.

They told me they had been to Wembley, but couldn't get a ticket under £80 and had watched in a pub instead.

They were so ecstatic about the game and just wanted to buy a Charlton supporter a drink to say thanks. They were stunned when I told them I'd come all the way from Australia just for the game and I had to refuse more offers of pints before making my escape to the Princess of Wales.

Brian Duffin had gravitated on automatic pilot to a different watering hole – one with its pros and its cons.

The rest is just a blur until we finally got back to Greenwich a couple of hours later and watched the game on Sky TV in Hardy's. More singing, dancing, crying and cheering. By half-ten the pub had run out of lager – I kid you not – and the day was coming to an end. One word – unbelievable!

David Hatch was apparently in a mood of mellowness, brought on by his willingness to stand back and take in the bigger local picture.

I went out at 8.15 to sample the atmosphere in the Charlton area and – wow! Cars all over the place with Charlton flags hanging out of the windows, loads of excited hooting car horns and the largest number of happy faces I've seen since the General Election. What a wonderful atmosphere of good-tempered celebration!

A tipsy fan in Charlton Village was standing in the gutter making happy victory signs to which a passing police car, catching the mood perfectly, responded with a quick blast of the siren.

People walking the streets around the ground were sharing laughs and jokes with complete strangers and a kid on a Lambretta screamed past the Royal Oak hooting furiously to

. . . reaction

the enormous amusement of passers-by.

The pub seemed packed solid so I went back to the British Oak in the Old Dover Road for a celebratory Courage Best. Very nice.

Rick Everitt might have intersected with David Hatch's path that criss-cross evening but, if he did, there's no certainty that he would remember. Although he does recall reviving, sort of, one old acquaintanceship.

We got a train from Blackheath to Charlton at about 11pm, none of us sober enough to consider buying tickets. The inevitable happened. The inspectors came down the train as it was about to pull into Charlton station.

They then proceeded to hide in the door recess. Yes, they hid in the door recess. Were we that menacing? Not at all. Well, perhaps we seemed so to one. One of the ticket men was former Valley shop manager Chris Tugwell!

Oh come on, Rick, pull the other one. You'll be telling us next that pigs might fly.

Father of less than a day Tim Bush paused in the West End for a pint before catching the next mainline train back to Brum. As it can do, one sip led to another and it was the last possible Virgin Express that he scrambled aboard.

It was 24 hours to the dot after acquiring paternal status that he returned home and came to appreciate the playing-it-long wiliness that underlay his wife Jane's matchday generosity.

No, the baby would not be named Sasa Robbo Clive Rufus Jonah Brownie and all the rest. Thomas William woud be quite sufficient, thank you very much, and, incidentally, had he got round yet to cleaning the oven?

Another metropolitan reveller was the aptly named Mad Milner, apt because he seems in pole position for the Valiant Gold Sword Award (UK Division) for the most dedicatedly sustained assault on the liver.

I have never been to anything like it in my life, probably never will. A superb game of football and Mend's hat-trick was something completely special.

Onwards to Covent Garden and the pleasures of too much alcohol. Half-past eleven and missed the last train. Not much more I could do.

How wrong I was. Trafalgar Square, singing and dancing.

Finally too tired to do any more. Head for Hyde Park for a game of football. Get warned off by the police so played on the streets instead, the adrenalin still pumping and keeping me awake. Lose our football and still three hours before first train home.

Decide to go on a sightseeing tour of London. Buckingham Palace and the rest, ending up in Brick Lane for a bagel. So tired from everything a taxi is required for the journey to Victoria. 5am. Finally, a train!

Home and to bed to prepare for the Woolwich celebrations.

Yes, if we may get a little ahead of ourselves for a moment, it had already been ordained that the festivities too were to go into extra-time.

Piquantly, not without a distinct dash of nerve, the same Greenwich Council that at the

Going up, going up!

Under escort

start of the 90s had been putting roadblocks and blockheads and vested interests in the path of Charlton's return to The Valley (OK, there had been two elections since, but six years is a short time in local politics), were on the eve of making good their promise to bestow the Freedom of the Borough upon their now favourite sons, win or lose at Wembley.

In time-honoured tradition a bus, the local heroes all but brimming over the side of its open top, would drive from The Valley to the town hall.

The event was covered for The Mercury by a writer not responsible for the rest of this section, Rick Everitt. It was to be one of the last pieces of copy he filed for the paper.

Poacher to gamekeeper. Completing – possibly squaring! – the circle, the once and still-to-be editor of the Voice of The

We're going to need a bigger mantelpiece . . .

Valley fanzine would soon accept the post of communications manager for Charlton Athletic and thus become a member of the Valley establishment.

Occasionally, over the previous ten years or so, his relationship with the club had known a strained moment or two. But nobody operating outside of the club's formal set-up – and you won't get an argument from any source on this one – had ever campaigned and argued more constructively or cogently to get the club back to its one true ground and up, up, up the Football League.

It's impossible to quantify his contribution to a revival that had led through Wembley to the Premiership and the honour being conferred the next evening.

But it is fitting that we allow his words to bring back Tuesday evening's burying of the borough hatchet.

Never had so many people waited so long for a bus.

Some had been in Woolwich since mid-afternoon. Others had been looking out for it since 1947.

Finally, the red double-decker carrying the men who had turned SE London into one big Valley party came over the hill at half-past six on Tuesday night.

As you'd expect with buses, there turned out to be two of them. First there was an open-top one to carry the players and VIPs, then another of more conventional design bringing everyone else.

Cheering crowds had lined the streets of Charlton to see them pass on the short journey from Floyd Road. But that was nothing to the jubilant thousands who packed into Wellington Street to witness their Premiership team's arrival at the town hall.

Eight remarkable years ago, that same venue had seen a bitter confrontation between the fans of Charlton Athletic and the councillors of the London Borough of Greenwich.

"No sandbags and helmets this time," joked former chairman Roger Alwen.

Certainly not.

Now we were all there to celebrate the return of top-flight football to London SE7 after an interval of 41 years. And for the club to receive the Freedom of the Borough, the highest honour the council could confer.

It didn't quite compare with the play-off final trophy Mark Kinsella had picked up at Wembley the previous day, but what the hell? The gesture was well meant and graciously accepted.

Now there was red and white bunting across the road, flags and banners. There were drums and singing, fans on every balcony and at every window. Cars hooted, pubs heaved.

Most of all there were happy smiling faces, belonging to councillors as well as the supporters penned in behind a temporary railing to ensure the buses were not engulfed.

Even the police were smiling as they took cameras from the crowd so that the fans could get pictures from a better angle.

"There's been nothing like this in Woolwich since the end of the war," said mayor Don Austen, a genuine native speaker with a politician's reluctance to hand over the mike.

He might be right. But it's time to stop looking back now, as manager Alan Curbishley went on to tell the assembled worthies inside.

When the bus left Woolwich two hours later, the crowd had dwin-

Haven't you got a straight glass, love?

It's the way I tell them! Radio man Mark Mansfield and chairman Martin Simons

dled to almost nothing. Two women stood opposite the town hall with a banner. It read only: "Our heroes."

But for every Charlton supporter, for good old Greenwich Council and even for The Mercury, it simply said it all.

So, for the second evening in a row the not very fertile twice five miles of ground around The Valley was punctuated by hooting (and, later, a little honking) and the sprightly sight of scores of cars, so many mobile clusters of confetti, belting about with Charlton flags and scarves streaming in their slip-streams.

For however temporarily, alas, the staid old suburban, commuter, solid-citizened atmosphere of London SE this and that was being transmuted into something altogether more precious. Into a mood that once, before the word was kidnapped, we might have described as gay. The local team had won and you might have been in Kilkenny or Parma or St Vincent.

One happy, happy Addick who didn't quite make it to outside the town hall was last night's heavy hitter, Mad Milner.

We last left him, gentle reader, crossing his threshold inwards at around six in the morning. He can speak up for himself as to what happened next.

Home and to bed to prepare for the Woolwich celebrations. Alas the phone seems to be constantly ringing to keep us awake. 4pm. Head towards the station. Time for a pint first. End product a party instead of Woolwich. The landlord was a secret Addicks fan and we celebrate in style. Sunderland fans join in too, wishing us all the best. Time to go home, finally. Arrived. Bed. The perfect end to the perfect Bank Holiday weekend.

And so say all of us . . . although, as we shall now see, Mad Milner was not the only one guilty of a certain degree of absenteeism.

THE ABSENTEES
NOT BEING THERE (1): Home

It's easy enough to calculate how many Charlton fans, give or take, were inside Wembley stadium on the afternoon of May 25th, 1998.

It's a lot harder to calculate how many fans, sort of fans, friends of fans, "I once went to a game at The Valley" fans were simultaneously keeping track of the game.

As we shall see, for many stuck abroad it became a case of suffering the tortures of the semi-damned cast into outer limbo. But since within the UK both satellite television and radio were covering the match, if there was any sort of will at all, there was a relatively easy way.

David Barrett, for instance, got it all well together.

I wasn't at Wembley but in Sheffield where I now work, so I ended up watching the game in the local pub.

Apart from the game itself, which incidentally was the most efficient laxative I've ever come across, what struck me was the reactions of the other people in the pub.

I sat at the back, two seats away from a couple of Sunderland fans with a cluster of Addicks down at the front. There was some good banter all through the game, until it got to penalties.

Then one of the Mackems looked at me in despair, as if to say: "How much more of this can there be?"

I actually said to her: "No one deserves to lose like this, do they?"

She shook her head and went back to biting her teeth.

When Sasa saved the last one, I went down on one knee and prayed. I actually prayed in the middle of a crowded pub which was in uproar – or was it relief that all the tension was finally over?

Then I went across to try to console the poor girl. She was in floods of tears and I just couldn't think of what to say. I think I told her that I felt really bad about going up on penalties and she turned round and said something like: "You're the last person in the world I need to be talking to."

I don't think she meant it maliciously, but I knew what she meant.

The sympathy didn't last long. When I came out, I was dancing all the way home – and there's a bloody steep hill between the pub and my house. I was bawling my eyes out.

Someone said: "You support clubs for days like this." Too bloody right!

What really impressed me at the time – and it's come through since then as well – is that absolutely no one begrudged us the win. No one has said we don't deserve to be there. And everyone seems to think it was the best game played at Wembley for years.

Of course, there are pubs and there are pubs. That afternoon it

News reaches Mary Dixon – and friend – at Glencoe in the Scottish Highlands

All aboard for Woolwich: plc chairman Richard Murray keeps hold of the cup

paid to be a little selective. Richard Constable paints a picture which, while cautionary, is not without its heroic aspect.

After him asking me repeatedly, I had promised an elderly uncle that I would take him on a return to his roots visit to the North East over the Bank Holiday weekend.

He had been born in South Shields. Since that was 90 years ago I felt – much to the disappointment of my wife and son – that I couldn't let him down by cancelling.

Off we went, miserable as sin, a state made all the harder to bear by the knowledge that my uncle was totally oblivious to our misery. He is one of a rare breed – a North Easterner not remotely interested in football.

It was only when we arrived in South Shields on Sunday that we understood the topographical implications.

South Shields is to Sunderland what Plumstead is to Charlton.

Waving them off: the open-top bus leaves Floyd Road

Home truth

The area was festooned in red and white bunting and it seemed as if the whole population had only one way of dressing – in football shirts.

On the day of the final, we gave as many Sunderland fans as we dared the thumbs down. From the safety of a moving car. Not very brave, I know, but we're not mad.

During the afternoon my wife, God bless her, volunteered to take my uncle for a long walk along the sea front. Had she known that extra-time and a penalty shoot-out were on the agenda, she might not have been so willing.

In my eyes and my son's her hero status falls only just short of that of the Charlton players.

Tim and I headed towards Sunderland, found a pub with a big TV screen and mingled as best we could.

As we listened to the fans talking in the pub – about 150 of them – it sounded as if Charlton Athletic were just a minor hold-up on Sunderland's march into the Premier League.

At kick-off the sound was unbelievable, but it declined as Charlton seemed to be gaining the upper hand and ceased altogether when Clive Mendonca scored his first goal.

To be honest I couldn't quite believe we'd scored. There wasn't a sound. Tim and I exchanged a puzzled look, thinking perhaps the goal had been disallowed. The same thing happened every time Charlton scored.

On one occasion I attempted an awful Mackem accent so as to remark to my son how well Charlton were playing. As well as the gentle kick I received in return, I had to then endure the drunken glare of a Sunderland supporter for the rest of the game.

As it progressed and Charlton kept coming back, you could sense a change in the pub's atmosphere. They were getting worried.

When Sasa Ilic saved Michael Gray's penalty the place was like a graveyard. It was now that Tim and I appreciated the wisdom of remaining anonymous. All hell broke loose.

One or two glasses went flying and one individual had a stand-up argument with the TV screen. Unlike Charlton fans, who were regarding the season a success whatever happened at Wembley, Sunderland fans had believed that there could be only one result.

Not wanting to impose ourselves on someone else's grief, we took our leave to meet up with my by now totally exhausted wife and uncle.

The remainder of the week was a delight. The whole area was more like Eastbourne at three o'clock in the morning than a hotbed of football. Having to miss the big day at Wembley hadn't been so bad after all.

As my son had whispered in the pub: "Unbelievable, dad, unbelievable."

A clear case of charity earning its own reward – and compelling evidence that here are two Constables who should be recommended not only for the DVC (Distinguished Viewing Cross),

Lining the streets

but for further undercover work as well.

Mary and John Dixon also wrong-footed themselves with their holiday plans.

It was true that in pushing on far beyond Hadrian's Wall they had safely removed themselves from the threat of any knee-jerk reprisals, but by travelling just about as far as it is possible to go and still be in the UK they had also distanced themselves from most of the communication aids that Southern Softies take for granted.

There is only one town on the Outer Hebrides – Stornaway, where our tour started and finished – and next to no settlements, phones or TVs.

It was a desperate afternoon. There were few stops and little time to establish contact with my daughter, who was monitoring the game in London. The reports she gave seemed unbelievable. It was clear the situation was changing by the minute.

We arrived back in Stornaway as the extra time period finished and rushed into the only pub. They kindly switched the TV to Sky Sports 2. The bemused Hebridean locals were then entertained by watching us watching the penalties.

In their hour of need, many Addicks rediscovered that it was good to talk. Andrew Tattersall, a NatWest financial planning manager, was at Wembley along with several of his friends.

They were scattered, however, all over the place in individual seats. What short-term strategic policy do you therefore adopt in such circumstances? Natch. You reach for your mobiles and start networking. Yah.

Putting the old peripatetic dog to longer-range use was Allison Panayi. She was also inside the stadium, but her father – with whom she has attended Charlton games for 25 years – had managed to get himself left outside. Some way outside, in fact.

THE ABSENTEES
NOT BEING THERE (2): Away

At the very same moment that daughter Allison was taking her seat at Wembley, her father was climbing the walls in Los Christianos, Tenerife, where to his ever-increasing dismay he was discovering that the most exciting visual link to the game was nothing better than teletext. But he did have a mobile. And Allison was pluckily prepared to pull it off.

I was a bit downcast without my dad. As soon as I arrived I reached for my mobile and updated him with news of the team and atmosphere. I promised to call him back at half-time.

One up! I call dad to share the good news and learn he's sitting in the corner of an otherwise empty bar, pint in hand, enjoying teletext with a Sunderland supporter. I gave him a quick first-half report and hung up.

Disaster! We're 2-1 down. Shall I call dad? No. He'll know. The next half-hour is enough to turn us all into nervous wrecks. Then extra time.

Two more goals. Penalties. Finally we're all going wild. I reach for the phone, press redial and scream into it "We won! 7-6! Penalties!"

There's interference. Dad can't hear! "7-1! My God!"

"NO, DAD. WE WON! 7-6! PENALTIES!"

He hadn't known! He had thought Sunderland had thrashed us. He had nipped to the loo at 1-1 only to hear the Sunderland fan scream as their second goal went in and promptly abandoned the joys of teletext.

When full time had to be up and the minutes went by, he thought I was too upset to call him. Mum said he was unbearable, pacing up and down clutching the phone, willing it to ring.

He was overjoyed by my kick by kick report and became one very happy and drunk dad. He'd told everybody he'd spoken to in Tenerife how upset he was about missing the game and now every bar owner insisted he and my mum had a drink on them.

Me? I end up with memories of one of the best days ever and a very, very expensive phone bill. But worth it. It's a bill I definitely don't mind paying.

The sound of the Bugle Horn

Sunderland 7 Charlton 1. If Allison Panayi was reduced to a nervous wreck, her dad must have had a nervous breakdown. A very nervous breakdown.

Most dear to the hearts of those finding out that the future's bright, the future's Charlton, must have been another US-based Addick, Mo Emery, currently of a fixed abode in Princeton, New Jersey, the state which pioneered the annual club shop rip-off scam.

To paraphrase Chamberlain – no, not Tosh – we have here a piece of Emery paper in our hand.

Due to prior commitments I couldn't make it to the final but I did get to hear the game live in the United States. I had my sister in Bexleyheath put her phone by the radio whereupon I could hear Mansfield and Powell loud and clear on my speaker phone.

This made me feel as if I was right there with everybody else. Since then I have seen the tape and visually witnessed the excitement as well.

The 196 minutes to England cost me about £18. What a deal! What a steal! What a game!

Rupert Murdoch isn't quite as bad as The Sun consistently tries to make him out to be. His Sky-racket does to a degree requite the footie that feeds it and, if you've a bit of nous as to where you position yourself, his satellites do sometimes hit the spot.

Faliraki is one spot where there's plenty of nous and Robin Robin Rapley, essentially of Surrey but a temporary Rhodes Islander, made sure he was in the right place at the right time.

It's 5am. I've just woken. Wouldn't have slept at all but for my excesses of alcohol. Still can't believe it. Addicks in the Prem!

Twelve hours ago I was sitting in George's Bar, Faliraki, Rhodes. George, in his best West Indian accent, shouts: "Any Charlton supporters here?"

Couldn't let this opportunity go to waste. Hand in the air.

"Come on, you Reds!"

All 80-90 Sunderland supporters look round to target the Southerner's position.

The match gets under way and I'm already sweating!

Ten minutes in and a taxi pulls up. Out jump three more Charlton supporters – Chris, Joan and son, I find out later. Always someone late for the kick-off. Still, nice not being on my own any more.

Super Clive scores! All four of us lose all bodily control. The Sunderland fan right in front of me turns and says inaccurately: "He's a bastard Geordie!"

"Does that make any difference?" I ask myself as the euphoria subsides. Yeah! Actually it does help!

From behind the bar, George, who I'm beginning to suspect favours the other 90 paying customers, shouts: "Don't count your chickens until they hatch."

Fifteen minutes to half-time. Get my third – or is it fourth? – pint in. Just as Heaney's actually about to beat someone and cross the ball, the screen goes blank.

George shouts: "Sorry. Signal problem."

Slow hand clap from the Wearsiders. Picture reappears ten minutes later. Still 1-0. That's OK.

Half-time. Get another pint in.

Second half and almost straight away Sunderland are 2-1 up.

Unbiased George plays one minute of "Cheer up, Peter Reid" at full volume and confirms my earlier suspicions.

Super Clive equalises. Sunderland fan in front reiterates the point about Clive's parentage.

They go 3-2 up, but then we start playing a little better. I whisper to my son (sadly a Spurs fan): "If we get back to 3-3 we'll win" – and, funnily enough, I actually believe it!

Rufus scores! Dreamland. Sorry

Letting it all hang out

Plenty of room on top

– really can't stop myself going crazy now! Full-time whistle.

I'm buying the drinks in twos now! Can't afford to miss any more.

Extra time. 4-3. The whole of the rest of the bar explodes.

Clive equalises again! Parentage? Yes, I know.

Full time. Penalties! 1-0 to us. The screen goes blank.

Comes back on. 1-1. 2-1. . . 2-2. Screen goes blank!

Back on. Nerves totally shredded now!

5-5. . . 6-5. . . 6-6. . . 7-6. Sasa saves one!

Total silence in the bar except for four people running around like lunatics.

Sunderland in front takes it like I knew he would: "You'll be lucky to get ten points next season," he says and buries his head in his hands.

Do I care? Not really. We've got another shot at the big time. How does that song go, George?

"Cheer up, Peter Reid,
Oh what does it mean,
To be a Charlton supporter . . ."
Yeah. That's the one!

Another Addick playing away that day, so to speak, was Nic Knight, impaled on Ibiza by his holiday-booking wife's long-range failure to recognise sheer class when it has just made a present of three points to Stockport.

Nic woke on the morning of the glorious 25th, nervous as hell and resigned to possibly following the game only by radio. Home and away events, however, were to give him two results.

People in the hotel knew I was a fanatical Addick and I had to endure every patronising statement under the sun.

"Charlton have always been my second team; they've done really well for such a small club; Mark Hughes is too old and slow for us, but he'd be great for Charlton". But I did get the feeling that they

Thanks for your support

genuinely wanted us to win.

Everyone tried to keep my mind off forthcoming events until a Hull City fan called Steve shouted across the pool: "Nic, I've just been into town to find a venue for the match. You won't believe this, but this Spanish bloke said he's hired all the World Cup equipment and, lo and behold, it turned up yesterday.

"He said that if we took a few down to watch he would set it up – big screen, speakers, sun, beer."

What more could you ask?

How strange to find a Spanish bloke in Ibiza. But it all happened.

3:45pm. Seats with the words "No 1 Charlton fan, No 2 Charlton fan" are placed in front of a very large screen for my son and me.

"Pint, Nic?" asks Wayne, an Everton fan.

"I think I could manage one."

"Don't you move from that chair. We'll supply the beer", says Steve in my Addicks-at-Wembley top.

"Cheers, lads."

Out come the teams. Oh to be at Wembley. But I am here and we will win.

Nic's forecast proved to be correct. Just as they had in London, Charlton squeezed by Sunderland – it was 7-6 in a penalty shootout, actually – in Ibiza. He took success in his stiff upper-lipped stride.

My uncontrollable blubbering lasted two hours. Different things contributed to this – the standing ovation I received from all the hotel guests around the pool on my return; our dinner table being decorated red and white by the hotel staff; the numerous congratulatory messages left on the table.

This all made for the greatest footballing day of my life. I don't know I believe actually being there could have been more enjoyable. But I will never know.

Simply fan-tastic

Bet he turned down the quiche.

Not everyone got their co-ordinates with Murdoch's ironmongery dead on beam.

All around the vacationing globe there were foolhardy Addick holiday-takers who went spare trying to contrive some sort of "live" access – television, radio, Internet, teletext, Eileen Drewery – to the game.

Benno Lindblom may fairly lay claim to being the most fanatical – or downright insane – Charlton supporter of all. His allegiance stems from having seen one game at The Valley – the legendary 1973 1-1 draw with Walsall. Somebody invite him over, for St Addick's sake!

He did watch the game on television. Sort of.

The game was televised over here on cable, which I haven't got. But I'm able to tune to the right channel with sound only. So there I was, sitting in our living room with my replica shirt on and staring, swearing, praying at the tube which only showed the "war of the ants" for two hours.

Do I need to tell you what my wife, kid and neighbours thought of my state of mind?

No, Benno, there's no need, thank you. Unlike your telly, we've got the picture.

The experience of Maurice Geoffrey Gunn – no, not the best midfield trio Notts County ever had but a Charlton fan living in Cheltenham, naturally – was typical of that endured by not a few up, up and away Addicks.

He and his family were in Cyprus, but the vagaries of satellite broadcasting know no international boundaries. The time zones may differ, but the transmission problems will be universally bad for your health.

I think I may have been the first supporter to know that Charlton would be in the play-off final. A year ago my daughter-in-law booked our holiday to Cyprus. Fine. Then I realised the dates. I prayed all season for automatic promotion but it was not to be.

But let's face it. Better in the play-offs than not at all.

On the first day of the holiday I met a Sunderland supporter. "No problem," he told me. "Nearly all the bars in Paphos have Sky TV."

The great day dawns and we spend the day on the beach, the tension mounting. One hour before the kick-off we all leave the beach, the men heading for the bars and the women for the shops.

When I got to Paphos there were about 15 Sunderland and six Charlton fans running from bar to bar, all trying to find a television with the game on. Because Sampras was playing, Sky TV in Cyprus was covering tennis. However, we were told that once his match was over, Sky would be switching to the football.

So there we all were listening to the match on the BBC World Service and at the same time watching the TV with the sound off and willing Sampras to a quick victory.

Under such pressure the drinks flowed, accompanied by bowls of peanuts and popcorn. When Charlton scored the first goal, my mouth was full of peanuts. They went all over everybody.

My son jumped up and sent the drinks flying – lager and broken glass everywhere. At last Sampras wins. Huge cheers. No football. Sky has decided to stay with the tennis.

Groans all round, especially from the Sunderland supporters, who in any case had groaned throughout the first half.

The second half was a different story. Our turn to groan. What a game this was turning out to be!

Despair to elation and back to despair. In the middle of extra time the women returned from their shopping and were wanting to go back to the hotel for our evening meal as by this time it was nearly 7pm, Cyprus time.

We rushed to our hired car and I tried to tune in its radio but – calamity! – I could not find the station. I drove quickly back to our hotel where we rushed up the stairs – couldn't wait for the lift – three at a time.

I grabbed my personal radio and tuned it in – to Story Time!

Don and on: the mayor makes his speech

Crowd seen

I paced up and down the bedroom, in and out of the bathroom trying to shave, shower and get ready for dinner.

Story Time at last finished and there was an announcement that Charlton were winning 5-4 on penalties, but that the final result would not be given out until after the next programme – The Archers!

This was the first time I have ever listened to every word of the Ambridge epic.

AT LAST they gave the result that, in both senses, I had been waiting to hear all day.

Bedlam! I ran up the corridor to tell my son and I think the whole hotel must have known. I went down to dinner proudly wearing my Charlton shirt and was congratulated by several fans from other clubs – particularly, surprise, surprise – those from Middlesbrough and Newcastle.

Although they were so downhearted, even the Sunderland fans bought me a few drinks which, coming on top of those I'd already sunk during a long day, gave me one of the biggest hangovers I have ever had.

I have asked my daughter-in-law to arrange for our 1999 holiday to coincide with the FA Cup final. Get your money on Charlton.

Half a world away in Thailand, Richard Pool was able to follow the game clearly both in sound and vision. For a while. Maurice Geoffrey Gunn's hangover will shortly appear small beer on the Ralph Milne scale.

10pm – kick-off in Thailand. I'm the captain of the island rugby team. The clubhouse is a bar in the main tourist area. It's opposite the best mini-golf (36 really amazing holes) in Asia.

Monday is darts night and the bar was packed – over 80 people

Drum roaming

A quick hug for former Charlton laundry lady Audrey Hannant

and the game on live.

It was soon clear that this was no ordinary match.

Further, as befitted one in full CAFC kit plus balloons, scarves, flags and wig, I'd placed too many bets. The worst were with a die-hard Sunderland fan and a Newcastle man. With each of them I struck the downing of two tequilas per goal scored against our respective teams. Everyone knew it was going to be a 1-0 kind of game.

What with all the normal match-day booze and the added excitement of my praying to Sir Clive Mendonca, all the neutrals present somehow became vociferous Sunderland fans – though they loved the game.

The tequila thing was maintained all the way through the penalties – though by now I'd given my shorts away when Rufus scored and then my shirt when Clive got his hat trick.

When the Gray penalty was saved, I was so ecstatic I ran screaming out of the bar and down the main street wearing only my Charlton flag. Sailing high, I banked and vaulted into the crazy golf. I was finally prised out of the Pirates' Cave dungeon by two armed policemen with flashlights. I'd been singing in there for nearly an hour.

Back at Patong jail, a brave attempt to explain my behaviour was made by the rest of the club and the football-mad Thai police seemed to understand. Most of the island knows about CAFC's season!

They said they would keep me in jail until 8am next morning "for my own safety".

What perseverance in the cause of a gentleman's word! When the dawn came up like thunder out of China 'cross the bay, it must have brought with it the head-splitting mother and father of all tequila sunrises.

The letter is signed "Ooo Roo". This must either be the Thai equivalent of Richard or the nearest Mr Pool could get to that at the time.

Sorry, Mad Milner. As UK champion you put up a brave struggle, but the Worldwide Addick Play-Off Final Headbanger Award has to go to – who are you? – Ooo Roo.

Mature reflection should perhaps lead us to believe that the last case history is not entirely typical of your average Addict, local or far flung.

Perhaps we can get back on slightly more familiar track with a cheering anecdote related by yet another resident of Boston, Massachusetts – Peter Vickery.

On his Wembley-centred trip back to his roots Peter divided his time between relations in the West Country and Welling. His approach to Wembley was in the company of the West Country branch of the supporters' club.

Travelling up on the coach, my brother, his son and I were talking about the old pre-Selhurst days at The Valley and were wondering what had happened to the guys

Hall of fame

we used to stand with each week on the centre of the East Terrace.

Although we met them each game and chatted throughout, we weren't close enough to be "friends". One of these guys was a milkman named Stuart. He always came to the game straight from his round.

He'd always have his apron, fingerless gloves and money belt on. He was a real wag – one of the football crowd comedians who always have the right comment to make.

I bought Richard Redden's book last time I was over and there is that great aerial shot of The Valley. On mine I drew a straight line to the barrier we always stood at and wrote that I had stood at that spot along with, among others, the milkman Stuart, whom I hadn't clapped eyes on since both the Addicks and I left for foreign parts.

After the Wembley triumph I was heading for my sister's at Welling as I had a flight from Gatwick next morning.

When we approached Wembley Way my two brothers-in-law, niece and I were confronted by a phalanx of red and white. We decided to go back to the Hilton and wait it out for an hour or so.

We were standing at the bar chatting among every Mackem south of the Wear that day – they were extremely magnanimous, by the way – when I heard a voice over my shoulder addressing my brother-in-law saying what a great game it had been.

I assumed it was just another

About that parking ticket . . .

Carried unanimously

Addick looking for shelter among the red and white stripes. I looked behind me and at once did a double take.

Lo and behold, there stood the milkman! I couldn't believe it. Turned out he'd moved on to better things and had a company in Indonesia. He'd been staying at the Hilton for the game.

I'd come 3,500 miles from the West; he'd come 8,500 miles from the East and we'd met up again quite by chance at the venue that had staged the greatest game of football seen since 1966.

Well, given twin loyalties that had endured over decades and surmounted hemispheres, perhaps it wasn't entirely by chance. Twin loyalties, twin towers. The venue in obvious question was soon to prompt Graham Speller into correspondence.

As the Intercity 125 – sorry, I mean the Virgin Express from Birmingham – makes its approach to Euston, it starts to slow by a post office sorting centre and in clear weather a glance to your left brings into view the full glory of Wembley's twin towers.

The prospect has often given me mixed feelings. They represent the highest aspirations to football achievement.

Yet so often in the recent history of CAFC, while we were struggling to maintain our existence, they have appeared irrelevant.

On my first journey on that line since Charlton's famous Wembley victory, I could see the towers shining brightly against a sun-filled sky. A quite different thought came to me.

We've been there and won promotion and suddenly Wembley doesn't seem exclusive and distant. Our success there means we join all those clubs who mark Wembley dates in their calendars.

The twin towers now symbolise that Charlton can compete at the highest level.

One thing's for sure. It takes a lot longer to get from The Valley to Wembley than from New Street to Euston. But Graham Speller, let us hope, may well be right.

Certainly David Hatch, whom we last glimpsed quietly taking in the local Monday night celebrations, would not argue with him. For the moment we will leave him the last word.

I just can't help reflecting on how lucky we are to have had such a superb set of directors, players and management personnel this season. The roof's off the main stand as the extension work progresses.

Robinson's fit again and Mortimer is seemingly not far behind. There's a large slug of Sky money on its way which, better still, the club seems determined to spend wisely. It just doesn't get much better. Who says it's only a game?

Indeed. Jasper Carrott couldn't have put it much better. Or at all.

THE MORNING AFTER

The next morning Britain had need to resume its post-Whitsun place at work or in the dole queue. Scores of Charlton supporters lifted throbbing and unwilling heads from their pillows to experience a second or two of half-asleep disbelief.

It was all too good to be true. Too extreme to have happened. It must have been a dream. Then the rawness of their throats sandpapered away their incredulity. No, by God, it hadn't been a dream and they had been there to see it happen.

Later, as they reported to office or plant, colleagues congratulated and even applauded them as if they had had a personal hand in Charlton's triumph. Perhaps, however remotely, they had. Certainly, the odd Spanner in the works apart, there was a sense that, across the country, for 24 hours Charlton were everybody's favourite second team.

Jonathan Fowles was one of hundreds of Addicks going back to the Connex South Eastern commuter grind that Tuesday.

The sardine can of a carriage he crammed himself into at Hither Green bore no relationship to the red and white packed train he had boarded the day before.

But on the back pages of the papers to every hand, banner headlines extolled the new high watermark in Wembley history.

Jonathan found himself standing above two seated unlikely lads he speedily suspected of Palace affiliation. Even if this was so, they talked for a while in open enthusiasm about the match and the sheer nail-biting excitement it had generated. Then, inevitably, one of them voiced an opinion already being stated in some of the papers being rustled all around.

"No question, though," the one said. "Now they're in the Premiership, Charlton are really going to struggle."

Jonathan found himself leaning forward. "Excuse me," he croaked. "But don't you think that yesterday they showed that struggling is something they're rather good at?"

He says that he took the ensuing gobsmacked silence less as affronted indignation that he had transgressed the commuter commandment of "Thou shalt not make human contact" than that he had made an unanswerable point.

Richard Hunt, a Robert Lee of a playmaker for the Valley Party in his energy and vision, offered a more philosophical overview.

Jetting in from Prague on the eve of the match, Richard had promptly got down to grass roots by joining one of the coaches picking up at Plumstead Common. Now, back at his workplace hard by Wenceslas Square and the certainly best lager in the

Flagging up Charlton's success before the game: Prague-based Richard Hunt

world, he e-mailed this on to the Internet.

Eight years ago we adorned Greenwich with election posters for the Valley Party. One showed a picture of the 1947 Cup winners' coach with a load of kids running behind it. The strapline ran: "If the council have their way we won't see traffic problems like this again."

Right now I've got my copy of The Mercury. On its front page is that photo of an open-topped double decker: "Never have so many people waited so long for a bus," writes Rick Everitt.

Looking at this I feel a line has been drawn under a phase in supporting Charlton, a phase when football on the field took second place to other wider arguments, when people tried to be rational about supporting a football club.

Maybe it got to me.

I was one of those who refused to believe last August that we'd seriously challenge and who refused to believe when Curbs said "Well, we'll just have to win our last nine games" that we had a hope in hell of doing that.

The time for those kind of thoughts had passed, unknown to people like me. This season belonged to the believers. To Richard Murray, to Alan Curbishley and to people on the e-mail list like Ritchie Mr Positive (Richard Chandler).

How we scoffed at him as he told us week after week that it was our destiny, the promised land was just a few games away.

Where are you now, boy? Stand up and take a bow. And the drummers who banged their way into the consciousness of broadcast commentators and fans the length and breadth of the country.

And Mick Gebbett with his final, glorious, e-mailed call to arms before the play-offs.

You guys prepared me for Wembley. After so many years of adversity I realise I'd come to always fear for my team before a big game.

In the final minutes before the start, when they emerged through the fireworks, I realised I wasn't afraid for them this time. I don't say I thought they'd win. But I became a believer and bellowed my way through the finest Charlton game I've ever seen.

The heartache is over, my friends. Those epic scenes were the sort that happened to other clubs. Man U, Liverpool – even Sunderland.

And then on Monday I walked into Wembley and there were 35,000 of us, a dancing sea of red and white and our team thrilled the whole country. Finally it happened to us. It was our turn for our "dreams of impeccable merit" to be fulfilled.

Thanks to the Believers, this is not a time for concern or speculation but for celebration. And not only by Charlton's fans, who have displayed faith beyond the call of duty, but by everyone who values the game in this country.

Instrumental in the team's success: Mark Garvey and drum

It is typically honest of Richard to hold up his hand on the charge of being a Doubting Thomas.

But in all fairness to the lad, Brian, following the Addicks largely from the far distant banks of the Vltava, Richard had not had the privilege of seeing for himself the almost tangible increase in steel that the inspired acquisition of Mills and Youds had brought to Charlton's run-in.

Mills had brought much needed speed as well as clout to the defence, while Youds' reading of the game and degree of comfort on the ball had been prodigious. Alongside them, Mark Bowen concluded the season by getting back to his international form and deploying it throughout three quite outstanding play-off contributions.

The three were the latest – not, let us hope, the last – jewels in a quite dazzling string of moves by Alan Curbishley to strengthen the squad.

As it proved. Just as with the earlier taking on board of the two up-front players Mark Bright and Steve Jones, acquiring the three defenders was greeted with some very raised eyebrows by many an Addick "expert".

Bright (as Bowen later) was well past his buy-by date; no way you could get 90 minutes out of a powder-puff like him. Jones was a strong lad, fair enough, and pre-

Before or after: who can tell?

pared to put himself about a bit and, all right, maybe, if you rolled a through ball right on to his boot but – cheers! same again, mate – no way the do-the-business striker we needed.

Talking of which, why had we wasted precious money on Youds and Mills when we had a good enough defence and ought to be going after . . . well, you know, Mark Hughes? If he'd take a cut in wages, naturally.

Experts! In fact, using the two radically different strikers alongside Clive Mendonca in a series of brilliant local alternations, Alan Curbishley brought campaigns to remember out of both of them.

Bright with his constant elusive runs drew defenders after him all season, one reason so many goals were notched by bombing-through midfielders. He held the ball up, spread it wide, in many a move that flowed through him and didn't break down.

When he wasn't scoring in the air, his subtle heading – he proved a much better header of a directed ball than his taller predecessor – created plenty of openings, not to mention chances.

And just when a defence thought they had come to terms with him, he could make way for Steve Jones.

Jones was and is a touch awkward. But mainly for the defenders marking him. He almost marks them. Indeed, taking on the entire Ipswich defence during the ten men holding action at Portman Road, that's exactly what he splendidly did.

Where Bright is "seek me here" evasive, Jones is totally in the defender's face: "I'm coming past you. Through you. Holding you off, I'm going round you."

There's not going to be too much suave distribution from the back by a defender contending against Steve Jones. Despite his opening day goal, Jones took a while to find his feet with Charlton.

But he settled his nerves and ruffled feathers by banging in goal after goal during that loan period with Bournemouth and then brought the recaptured habit back with him to The Valley.

Like Bright, given an opening, he can score with head or foot. Like Bright he contributed a vital top-up of strikes to the steadily mounting Mendonca tally.

And what must have pleased Alan Curbishley as most vindicating his judgement was that in the absence of Super Clive – as at Maine Road – Mark Bright and Steve Jones's differing talents dovetailed together very nicely, thank you.

To a degree they were gunning for the same starting spot. But Bright's cross to set up Jones's injury-time equaliser against City summed up not only their respective skills but their professional togetherness.

There may have been a "learning Curbs" period, but the Charlton manager's latterday dips into the transfer market have been as pure gold to the club. In fact, thinking about it, delete the "as".

At the time Richard Hunt was tapping out his reflections, Peter Bertram had even more reason to be taking the long view.

I'd known Bernie for about 20 years. He had a workshop up the alley from mine in Brockley. He was a self-employed metal worker. We always talked about Charlton. Like me, he had supported them from boyhood.

I saw my first ever match at The Valley in December 1962. It was against Chelsea and we lost 4-1. Bernie was older and could remember big games with big gates in the First Division.

He was the sort of man who would always do you a favour if he could.

"Have you got a ticket for Wembley, Pete?" he asked.

"Yes thanks, Bern. I'm going with my cousin. He's a season-ticket holder and he got me one."

"I've got an old mate from Yorkshire coming down. He's about 80 now, but he's got to be there so I managed to get us tickets. He's going to bring some programmes from the 40s as a thank you to the bloke who queued up for us."

I never saw Bernie at Wembley. I bumped into mates I hadn't seen since school (St Austin's, now a housing estate). What a day! We just would not lie down. My legs were like rubber during the penalties.

The Friday after the match, my brother said: "I'm knackered catching up after another bloody Bank Holiday, let's knock off."

"OK", I said. "But I've got to pop up the alley to have a word with Bernie."

When we saw each other a huge smile spread over both our faces. We talked about the game, about his 80-year-old mate, about getting home after the game, about next season.

On Saturday, June 6th, after a Saturday morning at his workshop and an afternoon watching the first Test match, Bernie died.

He was 65 years old, a decent, honest man who loved his family and work and Charlton. The last game he ever saw the Addicks play was the play-off final.

I'm getting a season ticket and when we play Arsenal and Man U and Liverpool and the rest, I will be there. And with me will be my friend Bernie. Although I knew him for 20 years, I still don't know his full name.

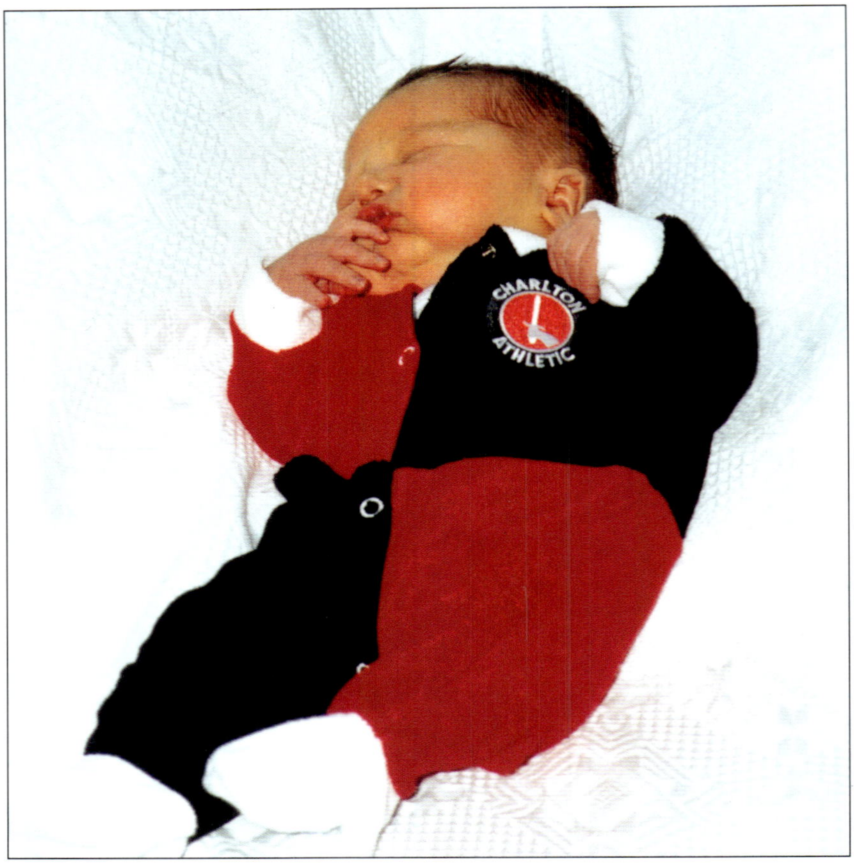

Thomas William Bush, born May 25th, 1998

In the midst of life. In this world Bernie will never meet Thomas William Bush or Emma Louise Diggins, born into Addick households on May 25th and May 28th respectively.

But may it be granted to all of us to go out on such a high.

And to be remembered with such straightforward affection by a mate like Peter Bertram.

In the days after the match – perhaps for a few even during its progress – people sought to make comparison with other titanic head to head encounters. Finnegan – Bob Foster, perhaps. Borg – McEnroe. Ali – Frazier. Liverpool – St Etienne.

Honesty and justice compel us to acknowledge that if a clash so memorable as to live on and on in legend is to happen, it must take two to tango, two to go the extra mile and then on beyond into that unknown region mapped out only by superlatives.

The same honesty now obliges us to acknowledge that, celebration of an Addicks red-letter day though this book is, it would be utterly churlish, utterly out of order, not to salute the magnificent performance of those who, almost by a technicality, walked back to their Wembley dressing rooms as losers. To take away from Sunderland's achievement is to diminish Charlton's.

The latter, it can be fairly said, have had overwhelmingly more than their fair share of bad luck over the past few years. Sod's Law has walked in through the Valley gates time and time again. On May 25th, the imbalance was in large measure made good.

For a start Charlton won the toss for "home" dressing room. A small point in the overall scheme of things, perhaps, and not as significant as them also calling it right for the privilege of playing in their first-choice strip – an area where Sunderland, by universal consent, proceeded to handicap themselves right from the off.

The sickly hue of the alternative shirts that Sunderland ran out in was not only unergonomic – how do you pick a man out with a long ball when he's half camouflaged against the sunlit Wembley turf? – but must have loaded on to the back of every player slipping them on a tiny nugget of demotivation.

Could this be a strip to dazzle in? If parrots ever are sick, this is surely the colour they produce.

More concretely, Sunderland were the unluckier side in terms of injuries. It is true that Charlton had John Robinson (recent hairline leg fracture) and Paul Mortimer (perennial hamstring trouble) at less than match fitness, but their substitutions in the course of the game were all cannily timed tactical top-ups.

Sunderland, by contrast, were forced to withdraw Darren Holloway at half-time on account of a back problem and, midway through the second half when he could no longer go on playing through the cramp and shin splint pain barrier, their key man Kevin Phillips.

Albeit with a lot of flirtation with the red card, Holloway was the one player who could be said to have got the better of Robbo at The Valley during 97/98.

The loss of Phillips for 47 minutes of open play – what if he had been presented with the one on one that Dichio fluffed?! – and, of course, for the shoot-out, might be said to be incalculable.

Understandably, the broken-hearted Wearsiders could not bear to stay and watch the ineffable moment when Mark Kinsella turned to raise the tin-pot cup (but just what did it symbolise and signify!) above his head and the carnival cavortings that followed.

They had already fled in droves. But if broken of heart they were no more broken in spirit than Peter Reid. There are dozens of recorded instances of Sunderland fans coming across to Charlton counterparts before leaving, shaking hands and murmuring from behind their tear-streaked facepaint: "Well done. Hope you stay up. Beat Newcastle for us."

They left the stadium to a choked-up murmur of sincere good wishes. "Thanks, mate. Your turn next year."

Such moments of respect and accord between two sets of emotionally spent supporters is best crystallised by returning to Gary Crawford's account of his day.

After the match I was completely drained – and we had won! Heaven knows what the Sunderland fans felt like. Then something happened that I had never experienced before that sealed a perfect day.

As I left the stadium there were still hundreds of Sunderland fans moving along the concourse.

They saw us, stopped, and began applauding, wishing us luck for next season.

Even on the way back home to Junction 13 on the M1, our allegiance instantly recognisable by two Charlton scarves flopping out of the rear windows, we were acknowledged by Sunderland fans with thumbs ups and waves. Incredible.

Then we read in the papers about the handful of morons that threatened Super Clive! It's not these fans that deserve the headlines, but the ones we met.

I wrote to Sunderland and told them of our experience and their reply is enclosed.

That reply was despatched on officially headed notepaper from the desk of Sunderland's corporate communications manager, Lesley Callaghan. It is perhaps appropriate that in a book celebrating perhaps the reddest and whitest red letter day in Charlton's history we allow it (almost) the last word.

Dear Mr Crawford,

Thank you for your recent letter and kind comments about Sunderland AFC.

Football is our passion but the game can deal some cruel cards. The last season has been an exhilarating roller-coaster ride for Sunderland supporters. We have witnessed some of the most exciting and entertaining football many of us can remember.

As a football fan you become philosophical and learn to take the disappointments with victories and that's what we will do. What happened at Wembley is now history and Sunderland Football Club will concentrate on what is to come, not what has been. Our experience only serves to strengthen our resolve and make us even more determined to succeed next term.

Sunderland AFC would like to salute all the fans that attended the play-off final and made the trip to Wembley an unforgettable experience. The support for both clubs on the day was absolutely tremendous.

On behalf of the club may I wish you success in the forthcoming season in the Premier League.

Amen to that. Come on, you Reds!

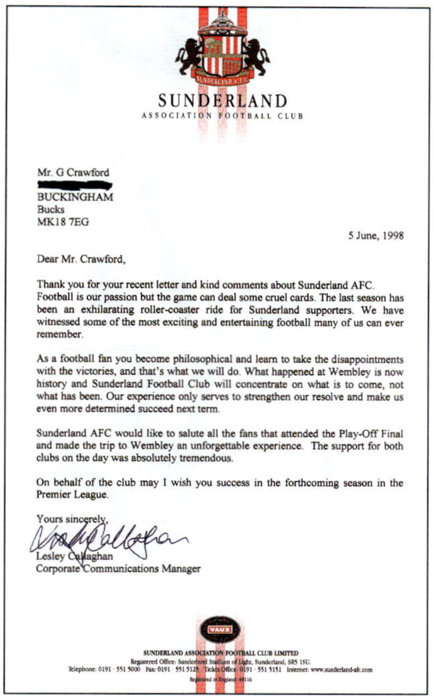

SUNDERLAND
ASSOCIATION FOOTBALL CLUB

Mr. G Crawford
[redacted]
BUCKINGHAM
Bucks
MK18 7EG

5 June, 1998

Dear Mr. Crawford,

Thank you for your recent letter and kind comments about Sunderland AFC. Football is our passion but the game can deal some cruel cards. The last season has been an exhilarating roller-coaster ride for Sunderland supporters. We have witnessed some of the most exciting and entertaining football many of us can ever remember.

As a football fan you become philosophical and learn to take the disappointments with the victories, and that's what we will do. What happened at Wembley is now history and Sunderland Football Club will concentrate on what is to come, not what has been. Our experience only serves to strengthen our resolve and make us even more determined succeed next term.

Sunderland AFC would like to salute all the fans that attended the Play-Off Final and made the trip to Wembley an unforgettable experience. The support for both clubs on the day was absolutely tremendous.

On behalf of the club may I wish you success in the forthcoming season in the Premier League.

Yours sincerely,

Lesley Callaghan
Corporate Communications Manager

VAUX

SUNDERLAND ASSOCIATION FOOTBALL CLUB LIMITED
Registered Office: Sunderland Stadium of Light, Sunderland, SR5 1SU.
Telephone: 0191 · 551 5000 Fax: 0191 · 551 5128 Ticket Office: 0191 · 551 5151 Internet: www.sunderland-afc.com
Registered in England: 49116

Good sports

AFTERWORD

The two unlikely lads on the train in to Charing Cross the morning after were, until corrected, of the opinion that Charlton would struggle.

Writing four days later Richard Hunt urged that it was a time for celebration and not speculation.

But now, writing some weeks after the event, it is perhaps not unseemly to conclude with a considered glance towards the future.

The first Premiership game came quickly over the horizon and with each day that passed every Addick fan wondered whether this time next year his team would be bracketed with Barnsley or with, say, Leicester.

Each was confronted by the growing realisation that, to coin a phrase, Charlton had it all to do again. Initial hopes may have soared like the value of the club's shares. Thereafter hopes and share value probably moved in perfect harmony, both settling comfortably higher than their position when Charlton turned the corner into the homestretch of their last dozen Nationwide fixtures.

There were some tidy counter-arguments to hand, naysayers for the refutation of. For instance and starters: who won last season's Avon Insurance Combination?

Was it Chelsea with their two-tier, choose Hughes today and go with the Flo tomorrow, multi-international system?

Was it no less big-spending Arsenal with their own pan-European twin set of starting line-ups?

Was it West Ham, another side qualifying for the League of Nations trophy before they even kick a ball?

No, of course not. Runaway winners were Keith Peacock's team of home grown youngsters.

Perhaps there's no-one in the second team quite ready to mark Bergkamp out of the game, but you don't have to be a genius to reflect that Charlton must have had a goodly measure of strength in depth before they spent a single penny in the transfer market.

Not that they haven't. To the point of being a role model, Charlton Athletic FC has demonstrated that it is a well managed club in the widest sense.

The ground improvements that raised the capacity of The Valley from 15,000 to 20,000 had been budgeted for irrespective of promotion being won.

There was no need to earmark the much-vaunted Sky money – "the most expensive penalty miss in the history of the game" – for ground improvements essential for the confirmation of Premiership status.

Four distinctly tasty players were swiftly acquired for what at first glance seemed bargain fees. Their salaries are another, behind closed doors, affair.

It remained to be seen whether or not Curbs' golden transfer touch had deserted him but the best guess had to be that he was still on a roll.

Certainly, he now had a squad sufficient in both quality and numbers to face the absolute certainty of forthcoming injuries with reasonable equanimity.

Indeed, he had a squad where the use of tactical substitution according to the given state of the game could be a very positive string to his bow.

Just where, when and how Messrs Redfearn, Powell, Hunt and Royce would start their Charlton careers was a fascinating question – and the sort of problem any manager would like to have.

Royce or Ilic? Bowen or Powell? If things went very well indeed, deciding such questions as these might be the area of greatest "struggle" for Alan Curbishley in the season ahead.

That, no doubt, is to be very optimistic. But given that one, single, complacency-derived home defeat for Charlton in the league last year, there would not be a single visiting side this season who came to The Valley and did not expect to, yes, struggle.

One final thought. Charlton's first-ever Premiership game was away. At Newcastle.

When they emerged in heroic ten-man equality from this encounter with Tyneside's pic'n'mix and have a sulk and take away the Colombian you first thought of millionaires, another managerial wobble was set in motion and a deliciously apt gesture of friendship made.

This time two sets of red and white supporters had reason to be glad.

THE FACTS

Charlton Athletic

1. Sasa Ilic
2. Danny Mills
3. Mark Bowen
4. Keith Jones
5. Richard Rufus
6. Eddie Youds
7. Shaun Newton
8. Mark Kinsella (captain)
9. Mark Bright
10. Clive Mendonca
11. Neil Heaney

Substitutions
Steve Jones for Neil Heaney 65
John Robinson for Danny Mills 76
Steve Brown for Mark Bright 93

Scorers
Clive Mendonca 23, 71, 103
Richard Rufus 85

Penalties

Clive Mendonca	(scored) 1-0
Steve Brown	(scored) 2-1
Keith Jones	(scored) 3-2
Mark Kinsella	(scored) 4-3
Mark Bowen	(scored) 5-4
John Robinson	(scored) 6-5
Shaun Newton	(scored) 7-6

Bookings
Mark Kinsella 17 (foul on Gray)
Clive Mendonca 32 (foul on Summerbee)
Richard Rufus 43 (foul on Quinn)

Referee
Eddie Wolstenholme

Sunderland

1. Lionel Perez
2. Darren Holloway
3. Michael Gray
4. Lee Clark
5. Jody Craddock
6. Darren Williams
7. Nicky Summerbee
8. Kevin Ball (captain)
9. Niall Quinn
10. Kevin Phillips
11. Allan Johnston

Substitutions
Chris Makin for Darren Holloway 46
Daniele Dichio for Kevin Phillips 73
Alex Rae for Lee Clark 100

Scorers
Niall Quinn 50, 73
Kevin Phillips 58
Nicky Summerbee 99

Penalties

Nicky Summerbee	(scored) 1-1
Allan Johnston	(scored) 2-2
Kevin Ball	(scored) 3-3
Chris Makin	(scored) 4-4
Alex Rae	(scored) 5-5
Niall Quinn	(scored) 6-6
Michael Gray	(saved)

Bookings
Darren Holloway 9 (foul on Heaney)
Kevin Phillips 14 (foul on Kinsella)
Darren Williams 82 (foul on Mendonca)

Attendance
77,739 (a play-off final record)

THE PHOTOGRAPHERS

This book would scarcely have been possible without the contribution made by the three photographers who attended Wembley on the club's behalf.

Tom Morris has been a fixture on the Charlton touchline for three decades and there can hardly be a single fan who is unaware of his work, which has appeared in every local paper as well as the official programme, previous books about the Addicks and on the Internet.

However, an occasion such as the play-off final is well beyond the scope of one individual.

Tom therefore concentrated on the formal parts of the proceedings, the action pictures and the final-whistle celebrations.

The byline of Steve Bridge, the former club chaplain, will also be familiar. In the past he has often covered the club's youth and reserve fixtures, providing a back-up for Tom at big games.

He took the fans as his main brief at Wembley and managed to capture much of the essence of the occasion as a result.

Tom and Steve were both present in Woolwich on the Tuesday night to record that event, too.

Finally, Tony Mitchell does most of his main matchday work behind the scenes at Charlton, taking pictures of sponsors and presentations. At Wembley, he was working for the Kentish Times and he was also the photographer at the official post-match celebration dinner.

Thus we were fortunate enough to have literally hundreds and hundreds of pictures from which to select.

We owe all three cameramen a vote of thanks for their efforts, which combined have produced a marvellous pictorial record.

Tom Morris

PICTURE CREDITS

Tom Morris
Pages 3, 23(b), 25(b), 26, 28, 29(a, b), 30(a), 31(a, b), 33(a, b), 35(b), 36(a), 37, 39(a), 40(b), 42(b), 43, 45, 47(b), 49, 50(a), 51, 53(b), 54(c), 55(a, b), 57(a, b), 63, 65(a), 67(a), 69(a), 80(a, b), 82(a, b), 83(a), 85(a, b), 95(a), 96.

Steve Bridge
Pages 4, 6, 9, 10, 11(b), 12, 13(a, b), 14(a, b), 15(a, b), 16, 17, 18, 19(a), 20(a, b), 21, 22, 23(a), 24(b), 25(a), 27(a, b), 30(b), 32, 35(a), 38, 39(b), 40(a), 41, 42(a), 44(a, b), 47(a), 48, 54, 59, 60(a), 61(b), 64, 65(b), 66, 67(b), 69(b). 70, 71(a, b), 75(a, b), 76, 77, 78, 79, 81, 83(b), 84, 86, 87, 88, 94, 95(b).

Tony Mitchell
Pages 24(a), 35(c), 36(b), 46, 50(b), 52(a, b), 53(a), 54(a, b), 56, 58, 60(b), 61(a), 62, 68, 72, 73(a, b).

Brian Thomas
Page 34

Others

Pages 11(a), 19(b), 74, 89, 90.

THANKS

Steve Bridge

Tony Mitchell

The following Charlton supporters have had contributions incorporated into this book.

Ian Amis
David Barrett
Peter Bertram
Tim Bush
Brian Cassey
Richard Chandler
Mike Collins
Charlie Connelly
Ross Coomber
Gary Crawford
Steve Dennard
John Dixon
Mary Dixon
Dave Dowding
Caroline Dowding
Sarah Downs
Brian Duffin
Debbie Eade
Mo Emery
Rick Everitt
Mark Filer
Chick Fowles
Maurice Gunn
David Hatch
Chris Hickey
Richard Hunt
Nic Knight
Rachel Kleinman
Benno Lindblom
Richard Mehigan
Michael (Mad)
Milner
Hugh Murnaghan
Garry Nelson
Graham Newson
Kevin Nolan
Allison Panayi
Richard Pool
Steve Rabe
Robin Rapley
Tony Rand
Martin Simons
Graham Speller
Andrew Tattersall
Russell Taylor
Ian Vagg
Peter Varney
Peter Vickery
Jamie Watkins
Tony Warran
Bob Whitehand
Martin Williamson

And so has one Sunderland fan!

Nic Wiseman

CONGRATULATIONS!
ON PROMOTION TO
THE PREMIER LEAGUE
CHARLTON
ATHLETIC
Coca-Cola
Coca-Cola
Nationwide
DIVISION ONE
PLAY-OFF WINNE
MESH